Approach to Archaeology
is intended for everyone intereste
principles which lie behind the arc
approach to the human past. It de
the nature of the evidence available, the
techniques employed to recover and interpret
it, and the problems which confront the
student of extinct communities for whom no
written record exists. The application of
archaeological techniques to historically
documented peoples is discussed in
relationship to the written record. As far as
possible, the book is written in non-technical
language, to provide a background to
archaeology for general readers of all ages,
and for those with an interest in the problems
involved.

Stuart Piggott is Professor of Prehistoric
Archaeology in the University of Edinburgh.
He is well known for his brilliant field work and
publications on the prehistory of Britain,
Europe, South-East Asia and particularly India.

PLATE I. Sarsen trilithon at Stonehenge, showing details of surface tooling brought out by artificial lighting.

Harvard University Press

Approach to Archaeology

Stuart Piggott

McGraw-Hill Book Company

New York Toronto

First McGraw-Hill Paperback Edition, 1965

Library of Congress Catalog Card No.: 59-16950

Reprinted by arrangement with the Harvard University Press

Printed in the U.S.A.

8910 MUMU 7654

ISBN 07-050013-4

McGraw-Hill Paperbacks

CONTENTS

ILLUSTRATIONS

Plates

Figures

ACKNOWLEDGMENTS

THANKS are due to the following for permission to reproduce illustrations:

Antiquity (Fig. 9); Professor J. G. D. Clark and the Cambridge University Press (Pl. V); Dr. H. Godwin and the Cambridge University Press (Figs. 4 and 6); Professor W. F. Grimes and Kegan Paul Ltd. (Fig. 11); Mr. B. Hope-Taylor (Pl. VIIa); Mr. E. M. Jope (Fig. 12); Mr. E. M. Jope and *Ulster Journal of Archaeology* (Fig. 5); Lufthansa A. G. (Pls. II–III); *Proceedings of the Prehistoric Society* (Figs. 1 and 8); Römisch-Germanische Kommission (Fig. 2, Pl. VIIIb); Sir Mortimer Wheeler and the Oxford University Press (Figs. 3 and 7).

INTRODUCTION

THE recent popularity of archaeology has produced a surprising number of books for the general public dealing with various aspects of the study of the human past. Almost without exception these books have been about field archaeology and excavation, or presented the more spectacular results obtained by these means. But with one or two exceptions, there has been no explanation of what is involved in the archaeological approach to the past, nor of the nature of the evidence which archaeologists use, and still less of the relationship of archaeological studies to those concerned with other approaches to history.

It would perhaps be pessimistic to think that this reflects an over-riding interest in means rather than ends, in techniques rather than theory, in practical processes rather than intellectual problems. In the hope, in fact, that this view is a pessimistic one, and that a few people at least may be more interested in the ideas and concepts which direct archaeological operations, and which bring about the elaboration of techniques employed in the field and laboratory, I have written this short account of what at least one archaeologist thinks about his own discipline.

The book is addressed to the beginner who wishes to know something about the foundations of a subject in which he has become vaguely interested, and especially to those early in their intellectual career at school or in the university. I have tried to present complex problems as simply as I can, without, I hope, falling into the pitfall of assuming, or giving the impression of assuming, that anything, however involved, can be presented simply without distortion of its true nature. Many of the problems which I have had to touch upon are ones of great complexity, and just cannot be simplified without turning them into a different problem from the one first encountered.

The book is planned so as to discuss first of all the general problems which are raised by the archaeologist's view of the past, the nature of his evidence, and the processes of inference and deduction that can be applied to it. There follows a brief account of the main techniques and methods used, both in the field and in the subsequent interpretation of the material recovered, and then a review of the means whereby archaeologists construct their chronological framework when this cannot be obtained from historical sources. Archaeological techniques alone provide us with information on the non-historic, or prehistoric, past, and the special problems which arise in this field of investigation are then considered, and finally the application of the same methods to historically documented peoples is reviewed.

The ideas here put forward owe much to conversations with colleagues similarly interested in what really constitutes the discipline of our study, and above all to my friend, Professor R. J. C. Atkinson, who has added to my indebtedness by reading the text in typescript.

The substance of the book was given as a lecture course to teachers of history in Scottish schools in the Moray House Training College in Edinburgh in the winter of 1957-8, but in its present form it represents a completely new version. The content of Chapter I was embodied in the Philip Maurice Deneke Lecture delivered in the University of Oxford in November 1958.

STUART PIGGOTT

UNIVERSITY OF EDINBURGH

THE DISCIPLINE OF ARCHAEOLOGY

I HAVE deliberately used the word 'discipline' at the very opening of this book because of its two shades of meaning. In the first place, we usually use the word to mean the opposite of slackness and untidiness, to imply something carried out methodically and according to rules. On the other hand, when one refers to an academic discipline, the word has a slightly altered meaning, defining an intellectual study which has certain qualities involving the use of reason, judgement, deduction and so on, in a way which will not only elucidate the subject studied, but will help to train a person's mind to work accurately and economically, and as an efficient instrument, on any intellectual problem.

What is popularly called 'archaeology' has at the present time a widespread appeal to many people to whom 'history' (if you used that word to them) would seem something different, and without much interest. What I want to make clear is that archaeology is in fact a branch of historical study, and that far from being something that can be easily understood without much mental effort, it is a real discipline in both senses of the word.

As we see later on in this book, there has been much confusion in many people's minds between some of the techniques and processes of archaeology (such as excavation or air photography), and the study itself which they serve. This is to confuse means with ends. Again, it is frequently thought that archaeologists are only concerned with prehistoric peoples and their remains, whereas the techniques of archaeology can be used equally well (perhaps even better) in the study of communities with a written record. If we are to understand what archaeology is about, and what archaeologists are trying to do, we must begin by looking for a definition.

If we are going to study individuals, societies, communities or other groupings of people in the past, we have got to use various techniques which will get round the fact that just because it *is* the past, the people we are studying are dead, and we cannot go and ask them questions or watch their daily life. In its wider sense, the word 'history' covers all enquiry into the human past, from the earliest times to a few generations ago; in a more restricted use, it covers the study of those periods or communities in the past who used some sort of a written record. If we use it for a moment in the wide sense, then archaeology comes within its scope as a set of techniques for investigating the human past by means other than those of history in the narrow sense—in other words, by means which are not those provided by written records. It is concerned with material objects of human origin, whether they are great works of art or masterpieces of architecture, or whether they are broken pots and pans or the remains of the hut of a stone-using savage. Archaeologists are students of material evidence surviving from the past, of the tangible and visible products and achievements of extinct communities.

For societies which existed before the art of writing was invented in the Near East some five thousand years ago, or those which continued to be illiterate side by side with the higher civilisations (as for instance the British Isles until the coming of the Romans in the first century A.D.), this material evidence is all we have to testify to their very existence. For prehistoric, non-literate, peoples, outside the range of written history, the archaeological approach is the only one that can be used to obtain direct information. As we shall see, there are other means which can sometimes provide indirect information, but this is another thing, and is not the application of strictly archaeological techniques.

The sources used by archaeologists in default of written records form what we might call unconscious evidence, provided by the things made in the extinct communities they are studying, and surviving into the present. It is unconscious evidence because prehistoric flint implements, or Roman pottery, or medieval churches were not thought of as historical evidence by the men who made them, but they acquire the character of evidence when the archaeologist discovers, examines and interprets them. The archaeologist is really always making the best of a bad job, and trying to reconstruct some sort of history from material that sometimes looks very unpromising, but is all he has to work with.

The past being what it is, accessible to us only at second hand through historical or archaeological sources, its study naturally involves constructing some sort of a picture of what the historian thinks it looked like. He can never be sure, because he can never go back in time to make his investigations on the spot, so what he must do is to try to put together, from all the available sources, something which will be consistent with the evidence he uses, and account for all the phenomena he has observed as convincingly as possible. Now this is really the same sort of approach to a problem as that made by the scientist investigating natural phenomena. He makes a number of strictly controlled observations, or uses those made by other scientists, he looks for the underlying connections between them, and then tries to devise some hypothesis or theory which will account for the observed phenomena in the most satisfactory manner. In scientific language, he will construct a *model*, a mental creation expressing the relationships and arrangements—perhaps in a mathematical formula—which will best account for all the observations he has made. The model will be a 'true' one in so far as it does satisfactorily account for the phenomena, but you can have more than one model at a time, all 'true', and the devising of a new model does not mean that all the others have to be scrapped, though some may have to be abandoned or drastically modified in the light of new thought.

Ever since man started thinking about his past, and so trying to construct history, he has in fact been making models (in the sense we have just discussed) of the past of mankind, just as the geologists and physicists have made similar models of the past of the world and the universe before the advent of man, or before life existed at all on this planet. It is worth while our having a look at the way in which archaeology developed as a subject in this country, because we can then see rather better why we think as we do in archaeology today. An understanding of the history of one's own subject is a great help in thinking clearly about its problems. Since archaeology is the only technique for examining the prehistoric past, let us look at the models of prehistory that were constructed over the past three hundred or so years in Britain. We must remember, in the first place, that the idea of there being a remote past for mankind without any written documentation was impossible so long as the Biblical narrative had to provide the framework for all thinking about the human past—in other words so long as a theological model of history (and prehistory) was believed to be valid. With this, too, there came from the Middle Ages a mythological model for pre-Roman Britain, based on invented 'histories' of Brutus and other non-existent heroes. But by Elizabethan times, scholars were beginning to look at what we would now call archaeological evidence objectively, and this approach was encouraged by the development of scientific disciplines of thought in the later seventeenth century, and the founding of the Royal Society.

Two new models were now constructed, or at least sketched out, of which the first was really based not on archaeological evidence, but on that of written history, and interpreted prehistoric remains in terms of groups of peoples with racial names— Celts, Iberians and so on. This racial, or ethnic, model went on in use well into the last century, and one still sometimes hears it being used today (though fortunately not by archaeologists). Of course this is not saying that there were no archaeological objects made by Celts, but merely that Celts are primarily people who speak certain types of languages, and though they may make particular kinds of pots or houses, their name belongs to a linguistic model, not an archaeological one.

The other model was one developed in the nineteenth century to such a degree that for a time it superseded all others. This was the model based on a classification of the substance and form of prehistoric tools and weapons, and the techniques of their manufacture: it also involved a theory of simple evolution from one type to another. Basically this was a technological model, and is still with us, for it was the famous division of prehistory into Three Ages, those of Stone, Bronze and Iron. It is a very good model, taken side by side with others, but like all of them it has its limitations and drawbacks.

The important thing to remember about this classification of the prehistoric past is that it is, in the sense we have been describing, a model constructed by archaeologists to explain a number of carefully observed facts. The broad prehistoric sequence in Northern Europe (particularly in Scandinavia, where the Three Age system was first worked out in detail in the early nineteenth century) is in fact one in which stone, bronze and iron were successively used as the main material for edge-tools. But to talk of 'the British Bronze Age' is not the same thing as talking of 'the Roman Occupation of Britain'. In a sense, the Bronze Age never existed in the past. It is a piece of archaeological short-hand —jargon, if you like—to denote a stage of development within a local sequence, if that sequence is seen within the framework of a technological model. The Roman Occupation of Britain, however, took place between certain fixed dates, and was carried out by individuals and groups of people we can name. If you used the technological model here, incidentally, you could do nothing except to place the events in question within the European Iron Age.

You can see it from another angle if you consider alternative models which have been constructed in more recent times, in response to the greater and more varied body of information made available by increased refinements in archaeological techniques. Chief of these is one based on the subsistence-economics of groups of peoples—whether they lived by hunting and food-gathering, for instance, or whether they were settled agriculturalists growing a crop of corn. If you use this, you make what looks like a very significant division in the Stone Age, what used to be called the New Stone Age being an agricultural economy, while the Middle and Old Stone Ages which preceded it in Northern Europe were based on hunting and fishing as a means of obtaining food. But in the Near East, people who were not certainly food-producers with an agricultural economy seem likely to have lived on occasion in settled villages, which in an alternative model based on social evolution, had been thought to be characteristic only of agriculturalists with cereal crops.

The truth is that none of our archaeological models of the past, inherited or recently devised, seems capable of providing a wholly convincing picture of prehistory on its own; there does not seem to be what a scientist would call a general theory covering all aspects. Perhaps this is no bad thing. The more facets of the past we can perceive, the more likely we are to have a view approximating to a general truth. On the whole, the tendency among most archaeologists today is to try to construct for the prehistoric (or very slightly literate) past a model which comes as near to a historical framework as the differing source-material will admit. But the source-material of the archaeologist, and that of the historian working from written records, are two very different things, and our next task is to try to understand what the essential qualities of archaeological evidence really are.

All study of the past is based on the interpretation of the sources available—written or unwritten evidence—and the making of inferences and deductions from them. What you can find out is naturally conditioned by the nature of your sources: each type of evidence has its potentialities and its possibilities, but also its limitations and drawbacks. The evidence used by archaeologists, that of material objects or structures surviving from the past, has its own particular limitations. You obviously cannot find out from fragments of pottery, or from the post-holes of an otherwise vanished wooden house, what language their makers spoke, or what they thought about life and death, or how their social system was organised. That is to say, you cannot find out this sort of thing if you use the archaeological evidence on its own—and very often that is what you have to do, unaided by any other deductions. You may get near to answering these questions, but it nearly always means that you have to interpret the archaeological evidence in the light of inferences from history, or from the knowledge we have of modern primitive peoples.

In archaeology, as in other forms of enquiry into the human past, you have to be sure just what your evidence is, and above all you have to decide how to use it properly, and to the best advantage. This means, essentially, that you must make up your mind not only what questions you want to ask, but whether the questions are, as a philosopher would say, meaningful. In other words, you must recognise the limitations of your evidence, and frame your questions accordingly; it is not only a waste of time to ask nonsense questions, but logically wrong.

For instance, suppose you found a bronze axe-blade in a ploughed field, or in the course of excavating a site. To ask 'Was this made by a Celt or a Pict?' would be a nonsense question, because the kind of evidence represented by the axe-head can never tell you that sort of thing. But to ask, 'At what sort of date were axes of this kind in use? Was it cast and then forged? Was it made in an open or closed mould? Is it a type in fashion in England, Ireland or somewhere on the Continent at some particular time? Does the composition of the metal tell me where the original ore was obtained?'—all these are perfectly proper questions, and an archaeologist should be able to obtain all this information from the object itself.

When we say that the archaeologist studies the material remains of ancient man, and when we look at what these remains usually consist of in museums, or on an excavation, we must remember that what is really available for study is only what has survived from the natural processes of destruction and decay over the centuries. What we study is the accidentally durable remnant of human activities: we work on objects of stone, metal, pottery and other substances resistant to decay because they are so often practically all we have to go on. Flesh rots quickly, bones are rather more resistant, but not always so; wood and cloth and ropes, nets, furs, skins, and leather are only preserved in exceptional circumstances, as, for instance, when they have always remained quite dry (as in Egypt or Arizona), or where they have been under water out of reach of bacteria, as in many finds in lake-beds and peat-bogs in Northern Europe.

Sometimes the existence of vanished objects, and the use of certain techniques, can be inferred from indirect archaeological evidence, as, for instance, when we reconstruct timber buildings from the data provided by the plan and proportions of the holes dug in the soil to take structural uprights, or recognise the existence of agriculture from the scratches made in the natural surface of the land by ploughing, preserved by a patch of a field being covered in ancient times by a bank or mound. Again, we know a lot about the cereal crops grown by prehistoric man in Europe and Asia, and about the nutritious seeds he gathered for food, from the impressions of grains and seeds surviving as accurate casts in primitive pottery or the clay plastering of hearths. It is because of the patchy and incomplete survival of archaeological evidence that so many elaborate techniques have to be devised in order to extract the maximum of information from what does remain.

So we must remember that owing to the accident of survival we may sometimes have a very one-sided view of the life of past societies. The flint and stone implements of the earlier part of the Old Stone Age tell us something of the stone-flaking technology of their makers, but we can only guess at the use of many of the tools. We know too that objects of perishable substances such as leather, wood, bark or fibres must almost certainly have been made by the same people, just as they are by stone-using tribes of the Australian aborigines today, but a couple of wooden spears are about all that have survived. It is a sobering thought that an anthropologist has in fact watched some of these same Australian aborigines making and carving a wooden object (a spear-thrower) with naturally broken bits of stone: in other words, in anything but the most exceptional circumstances, when the wood would be preserved, these people would have left no recognisable trace in the form of material evidence. Archaeologically they would not have existed.

So much for the incomplete nature of the evidence which has to be used by the archaeologist. We have now got to consider what sort of things can be found out from archaeological evidence not only at its worst, but at its best. What can we hope to find out about non-historical communities, those without any written record, or without any reference to them by contemporary writers in adjacent higher civilisations? To obtain the maximum information, the techniques we shall discuss in the next chapter must be applied, both in the collection and record of the information in the field, and in the subsequent comparative study of the material obtained. Given the results from such controlled investigations, what interpretation can we put upon them?

A distinguished archaeologist, Professor Christopher Hawkes, considering this problem recently, found that he could divide the sort of information which could be obtained about prehistoric communities, using archaeological means alone, into four grades, which, as he said, got harder as you went along. You begin by being able to infer quite a lot about the techniques used by the people you are studying in making things, and in carrying out the various processes involved in their everyday activities. This may mean a lot of complex investigation, such as the techniques of spectrographic or chemical analysis to determine the constituent metals and impurities in objects of copper or bronze, or of petrological examination of stone objects to see what sources of supply were being used. But the answers can be obtained by a reasonably direct interpretation of the evidence, and will be proportionately reliable.

The next stage, or next sphere of information which can be obtained, beyond the questions of technology, is that concerned with the methods of livelihood and the basic economics of the people you are studying. If you have all the remains of animal bones which have survived from meals, and been thrown away on the midden or into a convenient pit, you (or, rather, a zoologist) can work out the proportions of the different animals that were considered fit for food (and indeed of the joints favoured). In communities relying only on hunting for their meat and game, there will of course be no bones of domestic stock; on the other hand, you can detect the proportionate amount of hunting that a group of otherwise agricultural villagers were carrying out. Similarly, questions concerned with cereal crops or the gathering of wild seeds and other vegetable food can be answered in favourable circumstances. Trace of the interchange of goods between one area and another can again be detected. All this, too, involves laborious techniques calling for the co-operation of the natural scientists, such as geologists, botanists and zoologists, but a great amount of reliable information on these aspects of man's life can be obtained by archaeological means.

But when you try to go a stage further, you are getting into considerably more difficult territory. You may have successfully established the existence of a village community, using bronze edge-tools, making pottery, growing grain, breeding cattle, sheep, goats and pigs, building good timber houses and burying their dead in a cemetery near the village. So far, so good. You have found out all this, and perhaps other things as well, such as the fact that they liked certain sea-shells for ornaments to such an extent that they obtained them by some means even when living a hundred miles from the nearest sea-coast. But how was the village organised—who owned land, was there a village headman or chief, did he rule over one or more villages, and was there someone in superior authority over him? How many wives did each man have, was succession reckoned through the mother or the father, did the man, or his wife, or his children, or all of them, wear the ornaments made from the imported shells? What language or languages did they speak, what sort of dances and songs had they, what kind of ceremonies and religious beliefs?

Now, these are a lot of important and interesting questions that one would want to ask about any newly-discovered group of people, and they are only the beginning of the study of the social structure and political organisation of a community. But they are desperately difficult to answer purely by archaeological means. Suppose in the village you have excavated, you find one of the timber-framed buildings, represented by its post-holes, is bigger than the rest, and set aside from them. What can you safely infer from this? The big man's hut: the village had a chief! But why could it not have been a temple? Or a communal meeting hut? By itself, the evidence just cannot tell you which. Even supposing there were some hints, such as the absence of any hearth, or of the litter on the floor usual in a dwelling-hut, that the building might not have had a utilitarian use, what then? It is a common joke among archaeologists that you call a thing 'ritual' when you have no idea what its function was. To say you have a 'ritual building' really does not tell anyone very much.

The cemetery might help you more. If you found that the most of the graves contained nothing more than a single pot placed with the dead, but that a few contained a good assortment of the dead man's or woman's belongings—tools and weapons, ornaments and jewellery—then you might not be far wrong in inferring that the cemetery was that of people who had a society in which there were marked differences of class, status or wealth, which showed itself in the way the upper classes were buried, with more objects to make a show in the next world than the rank and file. But supposing there was nothing to distinguish one grave from another, so far as funeral offerings went? A society in which everyone has equal status, or one with a religion which did not enjoin its followers to denote their rank by what they put into their graves? You see how the inferences are becoming more and more difficult to make with any certainty.

We have really already begun to consider the fourth and last stage in these increasingly difficult processes of archaeological deduction: the question of the religious institutions and spiritual life of the community we are studying. Here archaeological evidence on its own can tell us very little indeed, except for generalisations so broad as to be almost platitudes. Evidence for a belief in some sort of personal immortality is present throughout almost the whole of prehistory, but we have only to think for a moment of the religions of the world today which share a concept of this kind, but which differ from one another in almost every other respect, to realise that to say that we have evidence that a prehistoric community had such a belief is practically to say nothing worth while at all. We can make guesses (they are hardly more) about the significance of such things as the Old Stone Age cave-paintings in terms of hunting magic, or about some sort of sun-worship indicated by Scandinavian rock-carvings, but even here we are not using archaeological evidence alone. This is important. The deductions and inferences about the method of making a stone battle-axe, the techniques of casting a bronze sword, or the way in which a pot was painted and fired, are all made direct from the objects we are studying. Of course, we can also use what we know of similar processes of manufacture made by historically documented or modern people doing much the same thing, but these comparisons are not absolutely necessary. But when we start interpreting the Palaeolithic paintings or the Bronze Age rock-carvings, we are using analogies, comparable situations, from primitive peoples whose beliefs are known or recorded.

In these last paragraphs we have been thinking of archaeological evidence on its own, unaided by any sort of history, however much at second hand. And with this sort of archaelogical evidence, we have got to confess, quite frankly, that the information we can derive from it is strictly limited. Furthermore, it would be logically wrong and a waste of time to try to get from this evidence information that in its nature it cannot give. If historical events, the social structure of communities, their ideas and beliefs, are not reflected by or contained in this sort of evidence, we must recognise the fact and confine ourselves to recovering the information it can in fact give.

On the other hand, as we shall see, if we are to make a distinction between 'text-free' and 'text-aided' archaeology (and it is a very valuable distinction to make), we shall find that a great deal of what is usually called 'prehistoric archaeology' is really dealing with communities which, because they existed side by side with higher civilisations which were literate and with an historical record, can be indirectly illuminated by written sources. With them we can, by combining strictly archaelogical evidence with that from other sources, get far further.

So much then for some general principles governing archaeological thinking, and depending largely on the recognition of the real nature of archaeological evidence. Now how does archaeology work operationally, how does the archaeologist set about his business of investigating the past by his own set of techniques? The first thing, of course, is the recovery, recognition and record of evidence of the kind we have been discussing in theory. This may either involve obtaining some brand-new information by field-work or excavation, or it may mean using material already recovered and preserved in museums or published in books and journals, or it may mean using all of them together.

On the whole, the evidence used by the archaeologist falls into two main classes of what we may call primary sources, each with its own group of secondary sources. In the first class comes information elicited by the researcher in person, either from field investigation not involving digging, or from excavation. This is a primary source, and one fundamental to all archaeological research. In its secondary form, it consists of the reports of such field-work or excavation conducted and published by other workers, and of course in this form it is much simpler and quicker to utilise than carrying out the excavations themselves. You can analyse the results of half a dozen excavations in the course of a morning's work in your study, but to carry out a single one of them may well have taken a whole team a couple of months or more.

The second class of evidence is what we may call museum material—the results of other people's excavations, or chance finds of objects, preserved in archaeological collections. These are primary sources in much the same way that original manuscripts in archives or libraries are primary sources for historians. Their secondary aspect, like the excavations in the first group of evidence, is when they are published in the form of illustrated catalogues or lists—this is like the printed volumes of manuscript sources in historical research.

We shall have more to say about the technique of excavation in the next chapter, but it is obvious that the value of the evidence provided by an excavation is in proportion to the skill and capacity of the excavator who did the work. If the dig was badly done, by someone not fully competent to undertake it, the evidence from it has to be regarded as suspect. This makes a very real difficulty for the archaeologist working on other people's excavation reports. In his own country, and in the circle of excavators he knows personally, he is able to make a mental (and very secret!) list of those of his colleagues he can rely on, and those he is not so sure about. Dr A and Professor X he knows to be first-rate field archaeologists, and he can accept their results; Mr B and Professor Y, however, may not be so reliable. But when he is using excavation reports from distant countries, and by archaeologists he does not know, he simply has to use his judgement as best he may, using the report itself as evidence.

It is sometimes thought that if an excavator was sufficiently painstaking to record, to the highest degree of objective accuracy, everything that could be observed during an excavation, his report would be an ideal document, placing its reader in possession of every fact, just as if he had done the dig himself. But this is not really the case. With the best will in the world, human observation is personal, and none the worse for that. An excavation is often compared with a scientific experiment in a laboratory, but the analogy must not be pushed too far. To think that archaeological evidence is of the same order as that used in, for instance, chemistry, is to misunderstand its nature, and so to try to apply the purely 'scientific' methods of interpretation will really involve one in asking just the nonsense questions that we discussed earlier on. What the excavator extracts from his dig will depend on his past experience, his comparative knowledge of the material he is unearthing, his quickness of apprehension, and a hundred other qualities peculiar to the individual. Obviously, the personal equation must be severely kept in hand; nothing is more valuable on an excavation than having at least one other trained and competent archaeologist with you all the time to argue out the evidence as you go along.

An archaeologist must also be an excavator, if only because it is by practical experience in the field alone that he can learn to understand the peculiar nature of excavation evidence, and so to use his colleagues' reports critically. He can also use the techniques of excavation himself to further his own researches. It is possible to be an excavator without having wide archaeological knowledge, but if so, an excavator with severe limitations. A good excavator must approach the site he is about to dig with a thorough knowledge of all sites of the same type; he must, in broad terms, know what to expect, and what to look out for. He has also got to understand his excavation as he goes along, for often each successive stage is determined by what has just been found, and interpretation of the features encountered can only be made on the spot, and in the light of comparative knowledge. Of course, each site is in its way unique, and often there is very little comparative information that can be brought to bear, but that does not absolve the excavator from the responsibility of knowing what there is to be known.

On the whole, the circumstances determining excavation tend to fall into two groups. The most satisfactory situation is when an excavation is deliberately undertaken to seek for the answers to some specific set of problems; the site chosen with this end in view, and the procedure of the dig governed by the successive problems—both those envisaged before the dig starts, and the new ones which inevitably arise during its course. On the other hand, much excavation has to be undertaken because there is a threat to destroy or mutilate the site—quarries and by-pass roads, housing estates and airfields, all may involve the excavator in a task not of his own choosing. Of course, new information of great value is often being produced by such 'rescue digs', but in their nature, and especially in the almost inevitable urgency in which they have to be carried out, they represent a far from ideal state of affairs for the archaeologist.

With regard to the second class of basic archaeological evidence, the material in museums, or available in published form, here again, of course, the original objects are by far the most valuable potential source-material. Much of the work that is being done by modern archaeologists on finds which may have been made a century or more ago, depends on the recognition of the latent potentialities in the things themselves, and the extraction of new information by new techniques. The methods of petrological determination of stones, for instance, the analytical identification of metal impurities, or the identification of seed-impressions in the surface of primitive pottery, are all examples of the way in which new information can be wrung out of old finds. For archaeologists, museums are the record-offices and archive-rooms of their subject. Here they can turn again and again to the original material, testing it and viewing it from new angles as new ideas and techniques are elaborated. And with any study which involves the consideration of large groups of objects related to one another by type or association, the publication of the contents of museums in accessible form means that much work can be done economically and quickly in libraries.

The archaeologist, contrary to popular opinion, does not spend his whole working life digging up treasures in the wilder parts of the world. Some of his work is carried out in the field, it is true, but much of it is done in museum, library and study, trying to understand what he and his colleagues have found, and how it fits into the pattern of previous knowledge. He has to spend a surprisingly large part of his time reading the results of other people's work; I reckon, as an archaeologist studying the prehistory of Europe and the British Isles, that I have in the course of a year to go through at least fifteen to twenty journals dealing with our own islands, and sixty or seventy covering the European continent. If you add marginal studies in history, philology and Oriental archaeology, the total would naturally be bigger, and, of course, does not include books and monographs.

Most archaeologists have to be specialists, however much they try to keep abreast of the main outlines of their subject as a whole. Obvious specialisations are the fields of Oriental or classical archaeology, or those within the Dark Ages and medieval periods of Europe. Even in prehistoric studies, though, there is too much to be covered in detail by a single scholar, and there are inevitable specialisations in for instance the Old Stone Age and its very individual problems, or within the second or the first millennium B.C. Again, one can limit oneself to the archaeological problems of a region or district, and pursue the story of human settlement there in detail against the natural setting.

In order to show how the archaeologists work, in fact and not in fiction, I am going briefly to describe some pieces of research carried out in recent years, one by myself, and two by Sir Mortimer Wheeler. One involved no new excavation, except as a sort of appendix; the others were dependent on excavation throughout, though never excavation unrelated to prehistory and history.

My piece of research really started long before I came into the story—in fact, about a hundred and fifty years ago. Attracted by the problems posed by the numerous grass-grown burial mounds or barrows on Salisbury Plain and elsewhere in Wiltshire, Mr William Cunnington and Sir Richard Colt Hoare joined forces at the end of the eighteenth century to carry out a major excavation campaign, which was spread over several years, and published in 1812. Technically, of course, the excavations were horrible, but they did produce a great number of objects buried with the dead, which the excavators had the wisdom to preserve in groups, burial by burial, as they were found. From their excavations, using direct archaeological evidence, they decided that they had been digging up the graves of the prehistoric inhabitants of Wiltshire, who had lived and died there some time before Julius Caesar arrived. 'We speak from facts, not theory,' said Sir Richard, but the facts he had obtained could not, in the light of contemporary knowledge, and within the framework of any model of the past then available, tell him any more.

But the evidence was preserved, and to it there was added during the nineteenth century other material of the same kind. All this material—pots and bronze daggers, beads and ornaments of amber, shale and other substances, objects too made of gold sheet—was in the museums of Wiltshire, Dorset and the neighbouring counties, or in the British Museum, and although there was so much of it, no one had tried to see what could be found out from it by a detailed study. We had got a bit further than Colt Hoare, and instead of saying it was Ancient British we said it was Early or Middle Bronze Age, but that was not saying a lot. And we now had some idea of its likely date, between 1700 and 1400 B.C.

The first stage of the detailed enquiry was to make a card-index of all the graves which seemed to be related by reason of the objects buried with the dead in each instance—what are technically known as 'grave-groups'. All the men's graves that contained daggers of a certain type, for instance, would be included; all women's burials that had beads of amber, gold or the artificial blue-glazed substance known as faience went in. Now this sort of card-indexing is not exactly an exciting process, and in fact it is often just a sheer grind, but it has to be done in order to assemble all the relevant facts in convenient form. With it goes the job of making drawings or photographs of all the objects concerned, so that you have them all available for comparison. In the end, you aim to have all the information in such a form that you can work on it without having to go any longer from museum to museum, and also in a form that can be arranged and rearranged in whatever way you want—you can bring together and compare all graves containing a certain type of pot, or you can reshuffle the cards and see what contrasts or correspondences you get when comparing all graves with cremated burials as against those with ordinary inhumations, and so on.

In the first stage of the work there appeared to be just about a hundred burials, all with features in common, and all unlike other Bronze Age graves in Britain. We now realise that rather more graves ought to have been included, but that does not alter the main conclusions made from the first hundred. What stood out clearly from these was that they were practically all concentrated in the region one could conveniently call Wessex, and that they were the graves of people who had been able to acquire in their lifetimes a lot of costly objects to be buried with them when dead.

Then, when one began to study the objects in greater detail, it became clear that many of them were either imports from the Continent or copies of imported types. This one found out by comparing, for instance, bronze dress-pins found in a few of these

Wessex graves, and practically nowhere else in Britain, with those found in contemporary graves or settlements in Europe—pins of a particular type were very abundant in certain areas of Czechoslovakia and Germany, for instance, and so the Wessex ones were presumably imported from there. Bit by bit, searching for comparable material in the archaeological books and journals, or in Continental museums, it became fairly clear that the people buried in these Wessex graves were in close contact with Central Europe and Brittany: it now seems likely that Wessex and Brittany both contained communities at this time which had strong connections with Central Europe, and were in fact probably in some sense colonies established from that region.

But that was not all that could be extracted from the objects in these graves. When one had accounted for things of local manufacture, and for those imported or derived from Central and Western Europe, there was a residue which included the blue-glazed beads. These must have been imported into Britain from the Eastern Mediterranean world, where the artificial substance of which they are made—faience—was extensively manufactured. Other things—gold-workers' techniques came in here—could also now be seen to relate to the same region. Here historical records, and so a system of dating in years, went back to very early times, and so we were able to connect prehistoric Wessex with the ancient history of the Levant, and pin-point our graves with more precision to a date centred on 1500-1400 B.C.

So by merely re-examining the objects dug up from Wessex barrows a century and more ago, it was possible to recover an important episode in British prehistory, one indeed of European importance. We have not finished with these grave-groups yet—we are just finding out where they got the stone for their battle-axes, and will soon be on the way to knowing more about the source of their copper, tin and bronze.

No new excavation was involved in this piece of archaeological research, but it does come in, as I said, as a sort of postscript. We realised that Stonehenge, with the great barrow-cemeteries of these Wessex chieftains and their wives clustered round it, must

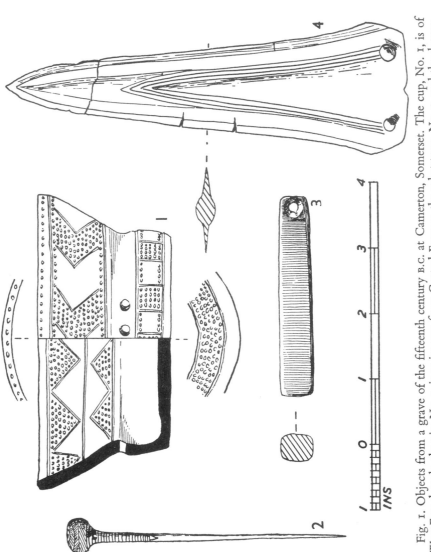

Fig. 1. Objects from a grave of the fifteenth century B.C. at Camerton, Somerset. The cup, No. 1, is of West French style, the pin, No. 2, is an import from Central Europe, the whetstone, No. 3, and the dagger, No. 4, are of local Wessex types.

have played a part in the complex story we unravelled in part. There had been excavations at Stonehenge, but the results of these only hinted at possibilities, rather than demonstrated anything clearly. So small-scale, selective excavations were carried out in recent years, and as a result, by the question-and-answer method of digging, we have now worked out the complicated structural sequence of the monument. And as we hoped, the final stone structure which we see in ruined form today works out as contemporary with the rich Wessex burials, and there is evidence that it, even more strikingly than they, shows evidence of Eastern Mediterranean contacts in its accomplished architecture.

The same process of reasoning from step to step on archaeological evidence can be carried out with an excavation programme, and Sir Mortimer Wheeler has demonstrated this line of approach on more than one occasion. When he excavated the great hill-fort of Maiden Castle in Dorset he found evidence that in the long structural history of the defences from about 300 B.C. onwards there was evidence for more than one point of contact between France and southern England. This deduction was made from evidence available in French museums and archaeological publications, but this was not enough. What was needed was field-work in north-west France, to see whether the characteristic fortification styles which appeared to have been introduced into Britain did exist there, and precisely where. Very little field-work of this kind had been done in France, and still less published. It meant going and looking for oneself. And then, if the field-work was satisfactory, it would be necessary to follow it up with selective excavation on question-and-answer principles.

The field survey was carried out, and the sites found much as had been expected and hoped from the available evidence. This was followed up by selective excavation at various forts, so that in the end not only was the archaeology of south-west England illuminated, but that of north-west France as well. Here the preliminary library and museum work led systematically to the field-work, and from this followed the carefully planned excavations.

Towards the end of the last war Sir Mortimer found himself, as Director of Archaeology in India, with a problem similar in kind though vastly more complex and far reaching. Large-scale excavations had taken place in many sites in the Indian sub-continent, but without any co-ordinated plan of research. One of the outstanding problems was the sequence of civilisation in south-eastern and southern India, and the relation of it to the large numbers of Roman coins found there. Was this trade or tribute or both, and what was its significance for Indian pre-history?

The first step, of course, was the recording of all finds of Roman coins or other objects in India in a systematic manner— the card-index again. This was followed by a museum-tour, to see what might be lurking unrecognised. This resulted in Sir Mortimer realising that a badly-conducted excavation on the Coromandel coast had in fact found a Roman trading-post of the early first century A.D., with characteristic pottery imported from Italy. He then turned to excavate this key site, established its stratigraphy and the sequence of not only of the Roman imported pottery and other objects, but the local copies of certain of the pottery types. Here was something that could be dated, even if Roman finds themselves were not present. And in the absence of any chronology for the region, this was a great step forward.

The next excavation campaign was in sites some three hundred miles away to the north-west; a city-site and a group of burials in stone-slabbed graves, of a type widely spread over south India. Again the question was one of dating, by going a step further from the sequence established in the Roman trading-post. It did in fact work according to plan. Not only did the native copies of Roman pottery turn up in stratified sequences, but a Roman coin of Augustus as well. Using these as a fixed point, the dates of the settlements found below and above the deposits containing them, and the tombs containing pottery of types which also occurred in the settlement, could all be put into their correct chronological sequence.

This process was taken up again, this time on a site seven hundred miles north-east, back on to the coast to the south of Calcutta. Once again the native copies of Roman wares were found, and once again they could be used to give a relatively fixed point in the local chronology. Because, of course, on each site the local styles of pottery, once dated by reference to the Roman datum, could then themselves be used, at a second remove, to give a chronological value to stratified sequences in which they occurred. The work initiated by Sir Mortimer in India continues, and by the theoretically simple, though operationally complex principles described, much of the story of the prehistoric and early historic past of the country is being pieced together.

These examples of what may be described as the routine processes of archaeological research serve to show how in fact such work is carried out. In the next chapter we will go further into the questions of the techniques used by archaeologists to recover and interpret their evidence, and discuss their uses and their limitations.

CHAPTER II

METHODS AND TECHNIQUES

As we saw earlier on, one of the qualities of archaeological evidence is that of being unconscious: we are dealing with things made by man which in themselves were never intended to convey historical information. The job of the archaeologist, in fact, is to discover the latent or hidden content of such things from the point of view of recovering or reconstructing the past from them. As a consequence, it is obviously necessary to devise means whereby such evidence can be discovered and recognised for what it is, and then, after discovery to elaborate further techniques for its investigation and interpretation. The evidence may not be, in the first place, obvious as evidence at all. A pattern of low banks on the Wiltshire or Sussex downland is certainly not immediately apparent as evidence of prehistoric farming; a thin layer of charcoal in a peat deposit cannot in itself be recognised as an indication of forest clearance by fire, and subsequent cultivation of the ground, though in combination with certain other circumstances this is exactly what it may mean. The nature of archaeological evidence demands the use of a whole set of complicated techniques in order to extract the hidden information.

Another factor which has also been mentioned is that of the accident of survival—the fact that so much of the total bulk of human craftsmanship and construction is carried out in substances which perish easily by decay and chemical decomposition. As a result, the more obvious remains surviving from the ancient past are likely to be those made of the resistant substances, such as stone or baked clay or metal. But the study of these alone would give at best a one-sided, at worst a misleading, picture, and the archaeologist must use all the resources at his disposal to recover

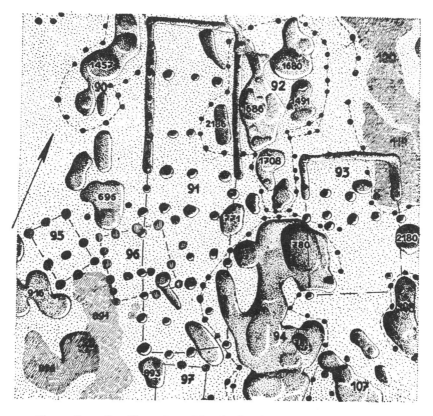

Fig. 2. Part of a village plan of the third millennium B.C. on the outskirts of Cologne, showing post-holes and bedding-trenches for long rectangular houses and square granaries of timber construction, as well as irregular pits and stake-holes.

something of the perishable materials of antiquity, whether directly, or by inference.

Timber-framed buildings, for instance, structures with a framework of upright wooden posts, have a short life in temperate climates, and will rot away without a trace on the surface. But to hold the upright timbers, holes or sockets have to be dig in the subsoil; smaller stakes will be driven in direct, like a fence-post. The positions of all these timbers penetrating the soil will leave traces in colour and texture even if all trace of wood has long ago vanished, and by the archaeological recognition of such features the plans at least of vanished buildings can be discovered. And from the depths and proportions of the sockets for the timbers, a reasonable estimate of the height and function of the original structural framework can be deduced, and so a three-dimensional reconstruction is made possible.

It is really then the deficiencies of archaeological evidence that have forced those who study the past by means other than the written record to elaborate techniques of far greater complexity than those necessary in dealing with documentary sources. In particular, as we shall shortly see, these techniques in many instances involve co-operation with other disciplines, especially those of the natural sciences. But although the archaeologist utilises these scientific methods, he does not turn his study into a science by so doing. The nature of his evidence, and the processes of inference from it, are not of the same order as strictly scientific evidence and inference. We might wish they were, but there is no good purpose served in pretending they are what they are not. Nor should we confuse technical means with intellectual ends. The elaborate techniques of the archaeologists are relevant and useful only in so far as they permit of the recovery and interpretation of archaeological evidence in terms of greater exactitude and detail than would be obtainable without such means. They do not dispense with the necessity of a lot of hard thinking when the evidence they have produced comes to be interpreted.

The techniques used in archaeology can on the whole be divided into two groups. In the first come the methods used in the recovery and investigation of primary archaeological material: its recognition for what it is, and its subsequent study from all possible technical aspects. In the second group of techniques we can put the processes of interpretation and co-ordination of the observed phenomena provided by the first group of operations.

The techniques of the study of archaeological material in the field are those which have attracted most general attention in recent years, and are those in which the archaeologist co-operates to the greatest degree with the disciplines of botany, zoology, geology, and the pure sciences such as chemistry and physics. The techniques involve processes of recognition, record, recovery and investigation, in varying degrees of simplicity or complexity.

The relatively simple processes involved in recognising the more obvious archaeological phenomena were, of course, applied from the very beginnings of antiquarian investigation. In this country, Elizabethans like William Camden were recording not only Roman monuments like Hadrian's Wall, but stone circles and earth-works as well. By the end of the seventeenth century some very good field-work was being done: John Aubrey at this time and William Stukeley rather later are among the founders of field archaeology in England, and their records still have a real value today. Both recognised the essential character of the process—seeing the remains on the surface, trying to form some idea as to what they represented, and then recording them by making a plan and drawing a 'prospect'—the equivalent of taking photographs today. The most difficult of these three stages, of course, was the second. The interpretation of the visible evidence of field archaeology in any secure terms only became possible slowly, as material was collected and collated.

In modern field archaeology, the recognition of visible evidence can be said to utilise two main techniques. The first is the most obvious and most ancient, as we have just seen—going over the countryside, identifying the monuments of antiquity, and making an adequate record of them. The identification of the nature of the sites, and their classification in terms of function or age, is made possible only by the background of knowledge of the prehistoric or historic periods represented by the remains themselves: in the early stages of the investigation it may only be possible to group them into arbitrary categories. The background of knowledge is built up from all the classes of evidence we are now considering, and is the product of the application of all modes of research and every type of technique available. The second technique of field observation is equally dependent on these factors, and is really only a shifting of viewpoint from the normal height of one's eyes to one more distant—this is the basis of air observation and photography.

There is nothing mysterious or complicated about the basic principle of archaeology from the air (the photographic aspect is merely the fixing of the visual record in permanent and portable form). The late Dr O. G. S. Crawford, to whom this technique owed its virtual foundation and initial development as an aid to archaeology, made a convenient and striking demonstration when he published side by side two photographs of a patterned carpet, seen (as he put it) first from the cat's-eye and then from the man's-eye viewpoint. The cat, a few inches above the carpet, sees a small area at a very oblique angle, which gives no indication of the structure of the total pattern, easily perceived by the man looking down on the carpet from a height. This is exactly what happens in air observation. Standing on the ground, the archaeologist may see that the ripening corn in a field is unequal and patchy in growth and colour (owing, as we shall see, to subsoil variations which may include those made by human activity); from an aircraft the total pattern is perceptible, and can be assessed in natural or man-made terms. So too with sites visible above ground—complexes of ruined stone walls, or banks and ditches, or the buried traces of structures beneath desert sand—these can to a large extent be planned, and their significance recognised, by the ordinary methods of field survey, but the air view gives, instantaneously and vividly, the whole lay-out, and may reveal traces invisible or indistinguishable to the observer on the ground.

The recognition that human activity may not only leave its traces in the subsoil, but that these may in certain circumstances be shown up by the differential growth of crops, was one of the most significant features brought home by air observation and photography. It meant that, over large areas of land where agriculture had destroyed all three-dimensional remains above the surface, the former presence of such structures might be perceptible, two-dimensionally, in the varying tones of a growing crop. In theory, the principle is simple enough. Disturbance of the soil by human activity, as in the form of digging pits (as graves, for storage, for sumps or for rubbish, for instance), or ditches (for enclosures or defences), or post-holes and bedding trenches for timber structures, means that though such features may be filled level with the surface, the soil contained in them is of a different consistency—usually looser and damper—than the undisturbed soil around. Crops with fairly long roots, planted over such subterranean features, will grow rather quicker, and so be slightly higher and darker green before ripening, over the disturbed spots, and this difference in colour at the right season of the year may be perceptible to the air observer, and can be recorded by his camera. On the other hand, where there are buried foundations of walls or paved roadways for instance, the crop will not grow so well, and so show lighter than that on the surrounding ground.

The same circumstances lying behind the appearance of these 'crop-marks' have made it possible to use a method of field survey whereby once again subsoil features invisible on the surface can be recorded without excavation. This, the method of electrical resistivity survey, depends on the fact that water is a better conductor of electricity than air or dry soil, and that in climates such as ours the ditch or pit or post-hole features just mentioned will contain, at most times of the year, soil moister than that surrounding them. So too stone or brick foundations will be drier, with more air-spaces, than the rest of the ground. If then an electric current is run through the ground between electrodes, bit by bit in regular lines over a surveyed grid, it will be possible to read off, and record, the electrical resistance encountered by each successive charge. When these figures are plotted to scale in their relative positions, one can join points of equal resistance just as in ordinary surveying points of equal height are plotted to form contour-lines. From these resistance-contours a plan can be made showing areas of low resistance, or high resistance as the case may be, and the existence of sub-soil structures of the kind described can be inferred. Of course, neither air survey nor resistivity survey can tell you the date of the structures (even if their plan may hint at their purpose and period), nor can it, in itself, distinguish between natural and artificial features beneath the surface. To interpret the pattern in terms of prehistory or history it will be necessary either to carry out some form of excavation on the site, or to interpret it less precisely by means of comparison with sites of similar plan and arrangement already excavated, and so assigned to a position in the known sequence of the human occupation of the area.

Before turning to the techniques of excavation, the most important and the most complex of all forms of archaeological investigation concerned with recovery and investigation, it is worth while pointing out in passing that, with the basis of knowledge provided by excavation and the subsequent interpretation of the material recovered, a large measure of elucidation can be carried out in the field without any digging. The relative sequence of complex structures, such as the defences of a prehistoric hillfort, can often be resolved into periods of construction and reconstruction by a careful study of the remains of its grass-grown banks and ditches, or its ruined stone walls, in the light of sequences confirmed from excavated sites. This process, of course, is really just the same as that used by the archaeologist when as an architectural historian he works out the structural history of the repairs and alterations to an ancient, or not-so-ancient, building.

Archaeological excavation, then, is the fundamental process whereby the basic material for subsequent study is recovered in reliable circumstances. Things may be dug up accidentally which can give much valuable information, but the circumstances of their discovery is not controlled, and may therefore be fallible. What is required is deliberate recovery and accurate record, followed by publication in such a form that the essential information is clearly set out in text and illustrations for the use of scholars. The excavator bears a very heavy burden of responsibility: as he excavates, he does in fact destroy the site he is investigating and, apart from the actual portable and removable objects he recovers, the essential circumstances of their finding will only survive in the form of his records. And so, as we saw in Chapter I, the amount of reliance that can be placed on the evidence derived from an excavation is in direct proportion to the competence and skill of the excavator. The use of often rather

PLATE II. Views of a patterned carpet: *below*, from the cat's view-point; *above*, from a man's height.

PLATE III. Views of a prehistoric site at Ogbourne, Wiltshire: *below*, as seen from the ground; *above*, oblique view from an aircraft.

complicated techniques in field archaeology today is not then just a love of gadgets for their own sake, but it is part of the process of ensuring reliability in recovery and interpretation. Fifty years ago, with the best will in the world, an archaeologist could do little more, if excavating objects from a peat-bog, than to record that they came from a certain depth, and perhaps to comment that there were ancient tree-stumps near them. But now, co-operating with the botanists engaged in the past history of plant-growth, he can ensure that, by the techniques of pollen-analysis, the precise position of the archaeological find can be related to a specific phase in the development of the local sequence of forest growth, and so fitted in to a natural time-scale.

When deliberate digging for more or less archaeological reasons began, people were on the whole concerned with finding objects, preferably works of art, that could be put in their private collections or in museums. We shall come back to this again in Chapter V. They did not conceive of the possibility of recovering details which could be used to build up a picture of the life and activities of the makers of these objects: indeed, in the prevailing climate of historical thought up to comparatively recent times, they were not very much interested in that aspect of antiquity. Unfortunately, this attitude is not extinct, especially in those fields where spectacular or beautiful objects or buildings can in fact be found by the process of excavation. Regrettably, but perhaps understandably, museums whose policy is to collect works of ancient art have encouraged this attitude in the very tangible and important form of providing funds to finance excavations in Oriental or classical lands, with an eye to acquiring objects that can make a spectacular show in their galleries. This is not to say that the finding of ancient works of art by excavation is not worth while, but it is surely wrong if the excavation is carried out simply with this end in view, and does not aim at as complete an investigation as possible, in which the works of art take their place alongside the other products of the community which produced them. For instance, despite the vast amount of excavations that have taken place in the Aegean and western Asia, we know almost nothing of the details of the domestication of animals during the periods of the great ancient civilizations, simply because the animal bones on which such a zoological enquiry could be based have been thrown away unrecorded in almost every instance.

Why then does an archaeological excavation take place, apart from those in the old tradition of treasure-hunting? And why, too, have we come to realise that more than portable antiquities can be extracted from the soil by such a process? The two questions are closely bound together, and their answers are really combined in one. The immediate circumstances of an excavation today are usually either that it has to be carried out in advance of the destruction or mutilation of the site by industrial or similar activity—a 'rescue dig'—or that it is deliberately planned as a piece of research to investigate certain problems. Whatever the reason, the concern of the excavator is to extract from the site he digs all available information within the limits imposed by the nature of archaeological evidence, and by the techniques currently available. He excavates to obtain information that cannot be obtained in any other way. The recognition that such information can be extracted by excavation processes goes back, in this country, not more than sixty years or so, and to one man.

Lieut.-General Pitt-Rivers, a forceful character and a natural genius, retired from a distinguished military career on inheriting large estates in Dorset and Wiltshire in 1880, turned his attention to the antiquities on his own land, and in a decade revolutionised field archaeology. When he started, excavation technique, as we understand it today, did not exist. You instructed workmen to dig a hole, in the hopeful expectation that you would find ancient relics—preferably you chose a burial mound, because the chances of finding pots and skeletons there were pretty good. You supervised these operations in a rather desultory manner, made a few notes if your standards were high, and carried home such objects as survived the assault of the labourers' pick-axes and shovels. But Pitt-Rivers, with an extraordinary grasp of all the principles which we now consider basic, suddenly, and entirely on his own, began to conduct large-scale excavations in what we would consider a wholly modern manner. Not only that, but as he dug site after site he improved on his own techniques, and became an even better excavator than when he began. Furthermore, he published his results with extraordinary speed and in a formidable wealth of detail which has proved invaluable to later workers.

The trouble was that all this achievement was practically ignored at the time. It was too much of a jump from ancient to modern in archaeological techniques. Despite Pitt-Rivers' work, and that which was going on along similar lines in other countries, such as Scandinavia and Germany, important sites were dug by important people 'like potatoes', in Sir Mortimer Wheeler's splendid phrase. And it was he who, in the 1920s, deliberately modelled his own excavation methods on those of Pitt-Rivers, and took things a stage further. By the 1930s, another development was taking place, derived from the Scandinavian countries, and involving the co-operation of the archaeologist with the natural scientists, such as the botanist and zoologist, and so making a study of man in his natural environment of the past possible. With the combination of techniques now possible, excavation in Britain was firmly set on the lines it follows today.

Excavation can be of more than one kind: an important division is between total and selective digging. Ideally, of course, the total excavation of a site is the most desirable, but the achievement of this ideal is hampered by many factors, notably the size and character of the site, and the time and money and persons available. For a burial mound, for instance, total excavation is not only desirable, but is relatively easy to achieve; for a hill-fort with complex defences enclosing several acres of ground it is still desirable, but hardly within our available powers possible to bring about. Research must be planned to make the best use of the resources at hand, and the respective merits of one total, or at least large-scale, operation, have often been weighed against those of a series of small selective excavations with a common object.

It is partly a question of aims. If we wish to study, to the best of our ability by archaeological methods, problems of economics and social organisation of an ancient community, then we want evidence for as near as possible the total lay-out of houses and other structures in a settlement, or all the graves in a cemetery. If on the other hand our enquiry is primarily concerned with determining the chronology and history of the site—when it was founded, what successive changes were made, and so on—the selective method will give one the main facts. Ideally, of course, we want to know both aspects, so that both types of excavation are necessary, and in fact they can be so organised as to combine to give a composite picture.

One of the basic concepts behind excavation was taken over by archaeologists from the geologists. This is the principle of stratification: the fact that (unless you stir them up) the discarded letters in your waste-paper basket will have earlier dates near the bottom, and later dates at the top. But the important distinction which must be made is that geologists are dealing with natural deposits, resulting from large-scale action which may be almost world-wide in its effects, whereas the archaeologists (except when they deal with humanly-made objects in geological deposits) are on the whole concerned with humanly-caused deposits which have a purely local sequence, and do not necessarily always obey natural laws. In fact, one of the things the excavator has to learn is how to distinguish, by colour, feel, texture and even smell, one layer from another in the accumulated deposits of his site, and to work out as he goes along the reasons for their occurrence. Only by this means, and by strictly relating his finds to the actual stratigraphy of the site, can he interpret the sequence of past processes, part artificial and part natural, which have intervened between the original use of the site, and the state in which the archaeologist of today finds it. This is why you will find, in any excavation, great attention being paid to 'sections': a vertical cut through the accumulated deposits of the site, showing them in their relationship one to another. Such archaeological sections can vary from a few inches to several yards in depth according to the site, but all have in common the fact that they show the

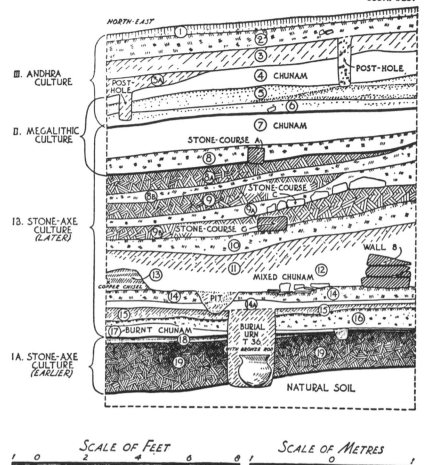

Fig. 3. Stratification interpreted in terms of successive settlements on the site, at Brahmagiri, Mysore State, India, spanning a period from about 500 B.C. to the third century A.D.

succession of deposits above the natural ground surface and below the top of the present soil.

The archaeologists's task is not only to recover the details of the site he is engaged upon, but to interpret these as he goes along, and to make a full and accurate record of them for the benefit of his fellow-scholars. As we have seen, it is sometimes suggested that provided an absolutely objective and accurate record of everything encountered in the excavation is made, it will be possible to understand it after it is all over, the site destroyed by the excavation process, and the information contained in an appropriate report. But it is very doubtful whether this ideal could be attained: it is even more doubtful if it is an ideal to be aimed at at all. It is in fact necessary for the archaeologist to interpret and understand his site at every stage as he goes along. You may make deductions which within a couple of hours will prove to be fallacious, but that is of no real matter. All you have done is to construct a working hypothesis which subsequent evidence shows does not in fact work. This is common scientific procedure, and you then go on to construct the next hypothesis which will take account of the new evidence. Bit by bit you come to a stage when all the significant phenomena observed on the dig can be explained within the bounds of a single set of hypotheses, and these in fact constitute the information you have obtained by doing the excavation. They have also to be tested, of course, against the evidence obtained on all the other excavations of the same type of site, with the necessary allowance for human beings not always acting according to a strict set of rules.

The purpose of archaeological excavation, then, is to obtain the raw material on which inferences and deductions can subsequently be based, under such circumstances of control that these should have a validity proportionate to the standard of excellence of the field-work. The raw material, the archaeological evidence, may contribute to prehistory or to history, or to both. Its contribution is the greater when it can be placed, from the outset, within some sort of a frame of reference. By this I mean that the excavation of an unparalleled or seemingly unique site may yield less information than one of a known type, just because the evidence recovered is of a wholly new kind, and, temporarily at least, cannot be related to an already established background of knowledge. The study of Roman Britain by archaeological means, for instance, progressed more rapidly than that of the prehistoric past, for from the first there was an historical framework of known facts against which the archaeological evidence could be placed. For prehistory, there was no outline, however general and imprecise, until it was itself built up by archaeological techniques. It is as our knowledge increases that we can see better how to employ our techniques, and to understand the evidence they provide.

A major step forward in archaeological technique was taken when it was realised that if the archaeologist worked in close collaboration with certain of the natural sciences, our knowledge could be advanced on such aspects of the past as man's relationship to his natural environment, and his degree of control over nature in such things as the domestication of animals, the cultivation of plants, and the exploitation of natural sources of animate and inanimate raw materials. In the 1880s, Pitt-Rivers had appreciated the importance of the study of the bones of the domesticated animals found by him during his excavations, in relation to those breeds still extant today; it was soon realised, too, that wood charcoal, which has a high survival-value, can on its cell-structure be attributed to specific species, and so give a clue to the botanical environment of an ancient site. The abundance of organic material preserved in the Swiss 'lake-dwelling' sites, known from the middle of the nineteenth century, had also provided a great stimulus to zoologists and botanists interested in the prehistoric ancestors of our present-day flora and fauna.

The systematic study of plant-life of the past, or palaeobotany as it is called, really starts early in this century with the work of the Scandinavian scientists such as Von Post and his followers, who demonstrated that plant pollen was highly resistant to decay, that the grains of the various species of plants had individual characteristics which could be recognised under a microscope, and that areas such as lakes or pools where peat was forming caught and collected a large proportion of the 'pollen-rain' in their immediate vicinity, and that this constituted a statistically valid cross-section of the proportions of the plants growing round about. If the normal geological (or archaeological) principles of stratification were applied to peat-beds (or other natural deposits containing pollen grains), it would then be possible to take samples at short intervals through the deposit, and determine in each sample the percentage of the various pollens, and so of the plants, growing at the time of the formation of that level of peat. Changes in the composition of the local plant-cover, whether caused by natural phenomena such as marked climatic changes, or by artificial interference such as that caused by forest-clearance by man, should show up in the successive statements of pollen percentages.

This is in fact what does occur. The Scandinavian techniques, extended to other North European countries including the British Isles, have in fact enabled a fascinating picture of the successive changes in natural plant-cover over the whole region to be built up, changes themselves reflecting major climatic variations broadly affecting the whole Northern Hemisphere. Co-operation between the palaeobotanists and the archaeologists has enabled these changes to be equated with prehistoric or early historic phases and cultures, and so some sort of a time-scale has been devised. In Chapter III we shall discuss the making of time-scales by archaeological means at some length, but it is worth mentioning here that the main phases in the plant-history sequence are now being dated independently by the application of the radio-carbon method, again to be described in the next chapter.

But one of the most interesting applications of this technique of pollen-analysis to archaeology is in the recognition of man-made alterations in the natural landscape indicated by otherwise inexplicable anomalies in the pollen count. It has been possible, for instance, to perceive in this country as well as Scandinavia, and on more than one site, a sudden decrease in certain tree-pollens at the same stage in the general plant-development sequence, but without any likely natural reason. When this is also accompanied, or quickly followed, by an increase in grass and cereal pollen, and in pollen of well-known weeds of cultivation such as plantain, the advent of human beings in the hitherto virgin forest, tree-felling and clearing land for agriculture, is

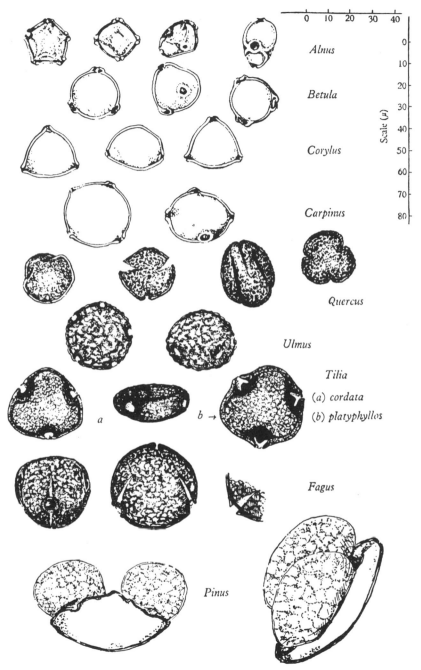

Fig. 4. Characteristic pollen-grains of common British trees. Scale in thousandths of a millimetre.

pretty convincingly demonstrated, even if archaeological evidence of just such activities was not also present in many instances. And when, as on occasion, this recession of tree-pollen is also accompanied by a layer of fine water-deposited wood ash, we can infer with some confidence that the forest clearance was being undertaken by the well-known 'burn and slash' method still employed in the remoter parts of Scandinavia.

So too, the pollen-analysis technique is telling us more and more about the conditions existing when burial mounds or other ancient earthworks were piled up so as to cover, and preserve for posterity, a part of the old land-surface contemporary with their making. Here again, one can detect evidence of interference with what would have been the natural plant-cover of the area, the botanical climax as it is technically called; evidence of adjacent cultivation for instance, or forest-clearance leading to the formation of heathland.

By the techniques of pollen-analysis and other means of botanical approach we can then find out something about the relationship of ancient human communities to the plant growth of the region in which they lived. The other main aspect of ecology, that concerning animal life in connection with human societies, is the concern of the zoologist. Communities whose life is based on hunting, fishing and gathering, are very closely connected with the animals they hunt or the fish they catch: if the herds of reindeer move to another pasture the hunters must follow them there, and the seasonal movements of shoals of fish similarly dictate the seasonal movements of the tribes whose livelihood depends upon them. In studying the archaeology of such prehistoric communities as these, the zoologist has materially helped the prehistorian, and enabled important deductions to be made about the subsistence-pattern of the peoples concerned.

For instance, lake-side settlements, evidently seasonal, and inhabited by hunters of reindeer, are known from several North European localities, and date from somewhere around 11,000 B.C. (the earlier) and 8000 B.C. (the later group). A statistical examination of the mass of discarded reindeer bones at these sites showed that the proportions of ages in the male, female and immature animals represented, when compared with the known breeding-cycle of reindeer, could only have occurred if the hunters were operating in the summer months, and so the seasonal camps marked the activities of the tribes concerned at that time of the year. On the other hand, a similar settlement of rather later date in Yorkshire (about 7000 B.C.), which might have been expected also to have been a summer camp, showed that the age-grouping in the bones of the food debris there indicated just the opposite, and represented a sample of the proportions to be expected in the winter. We shall return to these sites in Chapter IV.

When we turn to societies with an agricultural basis to their existence, and who have domesticated flocks and herds, once again the zoologist can provide invaluable information to the archaeologist. Indeed, the recognition that a prehistoric community has an agricultural status, with domesticated animals, depends ultimately on the zoologists' opinion of the bones which may survive from the site: this is particularly the case when, in the Ancient East, we are trying to pin down the change-over from food-gathering to food-producing, and attempting to perceive which communities were in fact hunting animals, and which had, in however tentative a degree, begun to domesticate them. Here again, age and sex grouping can be informative—a high proportion of ewes for instance may imply that they are kept for milking, and the bones of young animals statistically above the normal of average wild herds suggest domestication, since in hunting the larger and meatier adults will be sought after. And as domestication depends initially on taming the less fierce and muscular animals, and is followed by an easier life than that in nature, the muscle-attachments on the bones become less prominent, and other modifications of the skeleton separate the domestic from the wild species.

The foregoing techniques, belonging in origin to two branches of the natural sciences, are concerned with man's modification of nature by interference with the natural landscape or with the animal life of the region. But when we turn to man as a

tool-maker, and as a manufacturer of artificially shaped or com-
pounded objects, we can once more extract evidence from such
products of man's industry by the application of scientific techniques.

Two examples may be given, of which the first depends on the
fact that all rocks have individual and characteristic features
which can be identified and classified by means of examining a
thin section of the rock through a geological microscope. This
leads to the recognition of the various mineral components in the
rock, and their arrangement in the structure of the mass, and from
that the rock can be assigned either to a large and relatively un-
differentiated group, or not infrequently to a restricted type
which may even have peculiarities which ties down its source of
origin to a limited area. Since tough igneous stones were, before
the general use of metal, in great demand for axe-blades throughout the Old World, and since such stones do not occur every-
where, it is clear that a combination between archaeology and
that branch of geology which deals with the composition of rocks
or petrology, might give interesting information on sources of
supply and lines of trade communication.

A piece of planned research organised to investigate just this
problem has in fact been going on in the British Isles for some
years—the problem in its more local form being where did the
earlier stone-using agriculturalists round about 2000 B.C. get the
stone for their axe-blades when they did not use flint? We now
know that there were at least four main sources of supply—in
Cornwall, North Wales, the Lake District and Ulster—which
produced axes on a large scale at regular working sites on the
rock outcrops or screes, and that the products of these 'factories'
were traded widely into those regions of southern and eastern
England where there is no locally available igneous rock suitable
for the purpose. As the work goes on, more information comes
to light—for instance, it looks as though Scotland, although with
good rock supplies of her own, was importing quite considerable
numbers of axes from the Lake District and the Ulster workshops.

Work similar to that in the British Isles is also being carried out

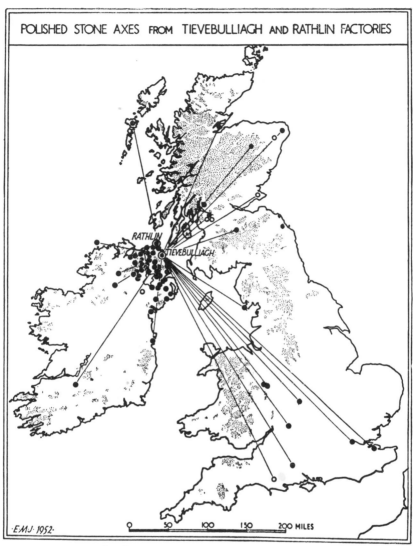

POLISHED STONE AXES FROM TIEVEBULLIAGH AND RATHLIN FACTORIES

RATHLIN

TIEVEBULLIAGH

·E·M·J· 1952·

0   50   100   150   200 MILES

Fig. 5. A pattern of prehistoric trade around 2000 B.C. plotted from petrographical data: an area of stone axe-blade manufacture in Ulster, and its exports.

in France and elsewhere, and, as we shall see again in Chapter V, the application of petrological techniques has also proved its worth in, for instance, the identification of the various types of marble and allied building stones used in the classical world, and for a similar approach to the question of the sources of the materials used in medieval buildings.

When one is dealing with substances such as metals or glazes, the application of the techniques of chemical or spectographic analysis of their composition constitutes a relatively obvious approach. In operation however it is by no means a straight-forward process, but one fraught with complexities and diffi-culties. However, the work now in progress in this country and on the Continent aimed at tackling, on an international front, the questions raised by the earliest working in copper and bronze in Europe, is already yielding results of great importance, and indicat-ing, rather in the manner of the stone implements but on a Euro-pean scale, the regional centres of early metal-working and the distribution of their products.

Only some of the main techniques of investigation have been mentioned: we shall encounter some others when dealing with the construction of time-scales in Chapter III. But recovery and investigation are only preliminary stages in the examination of archaeological material, and we must now look at the problems of interpretation.

Really, of course, we have been concerned with interpretation throughout. However elaborately devised the archaeological techniques, and however carefully they are carried out in the field or laboratory, they are useless unless they are directed to specific ends of interpretation. The evidence of archaeology only becomes evidence when viewed through interpretative eyes. We must remind ourselves once again that we are dealing with unconscious evidence, which only becomes significant when the right questions are posed. And asking the right questions is the business of interpretation.

To go back to ideas discussed in the first chapter, the form in-terpretation takes is to some extent conditioned by the conceptual model of the past which is being used, or, when using archaeological methods for historically documented societies, the knowledge already available from written sources. In the relatively recent development of archaeological method in Britain, for instance, we have already noted how the study of Roman Britain progressed more rapidly than that of the preceding periods, for the simple reason that the main historical facts relating to the Roman Conquest and Occupation were already known, and with the precise chronology provided by a system of coinage, sites and structures could be assigned to their appropriate setting. The question-and-answer process was for instance ideally applicable to the problems presented by Hadrian's Wall; it was less easy to apply the same methods to linear defences of wholly unknown date and context, such as Bokerly Dyke or Wansdyke in Wessex, Offa's Dyke on the Welsh Borders, or the Devil's Ditch on Newmarket Heath.

Part of the framework which is needed before fruitful interpretation of archaeological evidence can take place is chronological—within what local or absolute time-span the material under discussion lies—and part of it is a recognition of the type of society responsible for the evidence we are using. The question of chronology will be discussed in the next chapter, but it is worth while distinguishing here between two kinds of chronology. The most important kind is what is known as *absolute* chronology—that is, being able to work within a series of dates in solar years. This is to a greater or less degree possible in the historical past, which is historical just because it has some sort of written record which involves, or can be related to, a time-sequence in years. In the prehistoric or non-historic past, such absolute dates are more difficult to obtain, because they are not directly recorded, but as we shall see there are interesting ways and means of getting over this. The other kind of chronology is *relative*, as in the instance of having fifteen successive occupations in a settlement site, but being unable to relate any one to an absolute date. You may know that the settlement was rebuilt, burnt down, flooded, and replanned time and again after its first foundation on virgin soil, but you do not know how this is related to any historical sequence. Extreme cases occur when, as in the instance of hill-forts in more than one part of Britain, which on excavation have produced evidence of several successive periods of fortification and re-fortification, there have been so few significant finds that the translation of their relative chronology into an absolute one becomes wholly inferential.

What I have called the recognition of the type of society involved is a less precise affair than that of chronology, but it plays an important part in the interpretative process. You would not, for instance, expect the same material expression from a simple stone-using community with a subsistence based on hunting and food-gathering, as from one with a complex urban tradition involving an abundance of skills and crafts in many substances, including metal, and based on a farming economy. Again, the interpretation of the material remains of a literate, historically documented, society has necessarily to proceed along rather different lines from that of a community without any written record. The evidence at your disposal is not of the same nature in the two instances, and consequently your inferences are not of the same order. There are instances, too, where a group of related prehistoric communities may be represented either by settlements without burials, or burials without settlements: clearly the evidence provided by a grave is not to be interpreted in quite the same way as that from a house, since the conditions dictating the placing of objects with the dead man in his tomb are not, or need not be, the same as those governing the casual accumulation of refuse on a hut-floor or in a rubbish-pit. British prehistory for the period c. 1800 to 1000 B.C. has to be based almost entirely on evidence from graves and finds of implements singly or in groups; for the period of five hundred years before the Roman Conquest in A.D. 43 we have, outside a few restricted regions, evidence derived from settlements and fortifications alone.

The process of interpretation, as we have seen, is a necessary part of the intelligent use of the techniques of recovery and investigation in the field or museum or laboratory. The site recognised for the first time on the ground or from the air has to be interpreted before it has any significance. It has to be placed in a category, so that it can be regarded as illustrative of a general class, and not something unique in itself. Perhaps at this stage the categories have to be rather vague—a hill-top enclosure of a bank and ditch, a round burial mound—or it may be possible to be more precise—the hill-top enclosure may show features of plan and construction which excavation on other sites has shown to be a constant characteristic of hill-forts built by a certain group of people at a restricted period of time; the burial mound similarly may have features which would imply that it too could be placed in a context of time and affinities.

So too with excavation. Here the opportunities for making valid comparisons are of course increased with each new piece of material evidence that is produced. The more varied a selection of the material remains of a people, the more confidence can you place on inferences made from them, and much of the purpose of excavation is to increase the available material for study so that statistically it becomes more reliable than before.

Much of the process of archaeological interpretation is one of comparison, comparison between pieces of material evidence that may range from the ground-plan of a temple to the style of flaking on a minute flint blade. What is important is to establish similarities, so that pieces of evidence cease to be unrelated phenomena and fall into their place in the general pattern. This pattern is one of history or prehistory, and it is the business of the historian or the prehistorian to construct models (in the sense we have been discussing) which will indicate what appear to be valid patterns.

To take an example from the field of English medieval archaeology, we may consider the approach to the architecture of the Middle Ages in, say, the early eighteenth century. The only historical model to which medieval buildings could be referred was the vague concept of an age of darkness and superstition associated with the Goths and stretching from the end of the Roman Empire to the Reformation: all architecture within that period could only be classed as Gothic. It was only by the process of comparison and interpretation of the buildings themselves, here and on the Continent, taken into conjunction with the chronological framework provided by those whose date of building was known, that eventually a typological series was built up, from pre-Conquest Romanesque onwards, and ultimately related to the contemporary history of taste reflected also in such arts as sculpture and painting, as well as to the political history of the Middle Ages.

Similarly, a bronze axe-blade could, fifty years ago, be hardly interpreted beyond saying that (in terms of the technological model) it belonged to the Bronze Age; on its typology it could be said to be early or late in an assumed sequence of axe-blade forms. But now the process can give greater definition: the axe-blade is of Central European type, characteristic of schools of metal-workers operating in a restricted region and drawing on certain copper supplies within a similarly restricted chronological span; its appearance wherever it was found may be within what is known to be the range of the trade in such axe-blades, or it may be exceptional and unexpected.

The basic principles of comparison, and of the relation of one type of object to another, were worked out at the end of the last century by more than one worker, notably Sir John Evans in this country, and, most important of them all, Oscar Montelius in Sweden. The word 'typology' seems to have been invented and first used in this country by Pitt-Rivers, and denoted in fact the application of the systems used in the natural sciences to express relationships in the form and structure of organisms within an evolutionary sequence, but used for human artifacts. If you had a series of illustrations of motor-cars built between 1900 and the present day, you should be able to arrange them in approximately the right order—at least you would hardly put the 1958 Cadillac before the 1905 Renault. Why? Because it would be impossible to imagine any process among motor-car designers and manufacturers which, starting with all the features contained in the modern Cadillac, could by a series of modifications arrive at the features contained in the Renault. In fact you have what an archaeologist would call an irreversible typological sequence.

There are certain assumptions in the typological method which experience has shown are justified. On the whole, technological developments in tools and weapons follow the path of increased efficiency, and tend to work from the simple to the more complex. On the other hand, such a sequence must not be taken as inevitable. If a complex type is introduced from outside into a new region, its subsequent story may be one of simplification among people less well qualified to carry out the processes involved in the production of the original—this seems likely to have happened in more than one region of Western Europe where architecturally complex stone-built collective tombs around 2000 B.C. show local degenerations in size, complexity, and building competence. But on the whole, if the typological method is used with a due awareness of its potential pitfalls, it provides a basic tool of interpretation in archaeology.

The check upon typology, and the means whereby its scope can be extended, is the principle of associated or 'closed' finds. Objects deposited with the dead in a grave are excellent examples of closed finds—on the whole, the things concerned are all likely to be of the same date within a generation, heirlooms excluded. In passing, a really precious object like something made of gold may be more likely to be an heirloom, and so a generation or so old when put into the grave, than the common run of daily tools and weapons or pots. So if you find a pot of Type A, a bronze dagger of Type B, and a stone battle-axe of Type C, turning up not just in one grave, but in fifteen or twenty, you can reasonably assume that these three types were current at about the same time. Now let us suppose that in three or four of these graves there were not only Types A, B and C (either all three, or at least two, together), but that there were also bronze axe-blades, of Type D. This would mean that Type D axes were also contemporary, and if you then found in another region a lot of graves with Type D axes and also a new kind of pot, Type E, you could go a stage further and say that Type A pots and Type E pots, though never found together, were the products of two communities roughly contemporary in time, but separated in space.

This, reduced to such simple terms that it would be misleading if taken too literally, is nevertheless the way in which much of our picture of the prehistoric past is built up, and even to some extent that of the historical past too. Much of our knowledge of Oriental or classical antiquity, or of barbarian Europe after the fall of the Roman Empire in the West, is based on just such techniques of interpretation. What is built up is a pattern in two dimensions—time and space. The construction of the chronological dimension where none exists in an historical record is discussed in the next chapter, and we have already touched on its relative and absolute aspects. The space dimension is of course simply the geographical boundaries of what the archaeologist has chosen as significant groupings of types which seem to define the products of a single tradition within a community or group of communities—the equivalent of a clan or tribe or state in some form or other. It is naturally very important to be able to establish whether two such individual traditions are co-existing in time as well as existing side by side in the geographical sense.

What I hope emerges from all this is that what are usually thought of as the archaeologists' entire bag of tricks—the techniques associated with field work and excavation—are only part of the story. Unless they are used within the framework of an interpretative process they are useless and a waste of time and effort. This is the process I referred to in the first chapter, when I mentioned the large amount of research and investigation which has to go on all the time, in the historic or prehistoric field, or both, if the archaeologist is to make the best use of his techniques, or indeed to use them sensibly at all. These are necessary in order to ensure so far as possible the reliability of the evidence, but they may in fact fail to do this if they are not applied with a knowledge of their precise functions within the major discipline.

CHAPTER III

MAKING TIME-SCALES

ANY enquiry into the past which does not reckon with the dimension of time is obviously nonsense: the past *is* the past by virtue of the place it occupies in the time-scale. The archaeological approach to the human past has to concern itself with problems of chronology no less than that of the historian working from written records, and indeed the archaeologist has to spend a far greater part of his time in worrying out his time-scales than has the historian, because so often he is dealing with non-literate societies which of their very nature provide no direct evidence of their place in time. As a result, the archaeologist studying prehistoric, or non-historic, societies has to devise means whereby these societies can be put in chronological relation one with another, or with co-existing literate and historical communities with a time-scale of their own.

History provides its own time-scale, either precisely or approximately, in terms of what we have seen should be called absolute chronology—a time-scale with dates, not just a sequence. The absolute chronologies of historians are provided by various literary means, ranging from the evidence of epigraphy and numismatics (inscriptions and coins) to that of all sorts of historical documents providing conscious or unconscious evidence of dates. Given in terms of solar years and reckoned before or after the birth of Christ, these are our familiar 'historical dates', which vary in precision from, for instance, the date of the beginning of the reign of Henry II of England, which happened to be the fourth Sunday in Advent, December 19, A.D. 1154, to that of the beginning of the Eighteenth Dynasty in Egypt under Ahmosis, which was probabiy the year 1580 B.C., without our having complete certainty that it might not have been a year or so earlier. But even if there is a possibility of error of a year or two in computing the date for the beginning of the Egyptian New Kingdom, this is a reasonable enough fixed point in the second millennium B.C., and one of a quite different order of validity from the sort of absolute date we can arrive at by purely archaeological means for a non-historic community within the same millennium.

But nevertheless, the archaeologist and prehistorian cannot begin to work unless he has some sort of a chronological framework. In a recent book on the Early Bronze Age in Northern Germany the author opens with the decisive statement—'Prehistoric archaeology is an historical discipline'. And Sir Mortimer Wheeler said, in reference to the Indus Valley civilisation, that not so long ago we were in the position of having a railway guide which showed that lots of trains were running, but omitted the essential facts of when they started and when they stopped. Unless we have a time-table, in fact, and treat our material in terms of a historical and chronological framework, we cannot perceive the significance of the knowledge we have accumulated. If, in the field of non-historic antiquity, we have, by means of the various techniques of archaeology, collected and interpreted the evidence for the existence of a number of communities of people, and worked out their distribution in space, we cannot go on to understand their significance until we have also fixed their distribution in time. However much we know of their economies and their technologies, their art styles and their burial customs, their house-plans and their pottery forms, all this has a limited meaning if we do not know their position in time. Where does Community A come in relation to other groups of people who may have occupied the same territory before and after? And did it flourish at the same time as, or before, or after, Communities B, C and D? And where do they all fit in with regard to the historical civilisations of the ancient world? In the terms we have already met in Chapter II, what are their relative and absolute chronologies?

These are the questions which the archaeologist has to face when he is dealing with ancient communities which are either wholly without historical documentation, or in which the historical documentation is very scanty and ambiguous, and can only be used in close conjunction with archaeological evidence. He has first to establish relative chronologies, and then where possible, to convert these into terms of actual dates, or in other words to provide an absolute chronology. The approach to the problem is determined at the outset, of course, by the possibility that the communities he is studying from their surviving remains may either have flourished before any written history existed at all, or that at however far a remove in space, they were contemporary with some phase of the civilisations of historical antiquity. The dividing line of course varies—some sort of an historical framework exists in the Old World from about 3000 B.C., but this does not affect the archaeology of the American Indians or of the New Zealand Maoris, who can only be related to historically documented societies from the point of contact with European invaders.

We shall see that a recently developed technique based on the rate of the radio-active breakdown of a carbon isotope present in organic matter is now beginning to provide absolute dates which have a validity which does not depend on any correlation with history. This however involves elaborate and costly laboratory processes, is subject to errors still not wholly predictable or avoidable, and is not universally applicable to all archaeological material. Other means have to be employed in constructing time-scales, and it is by such means that our chronological framework for prehistoric peoples has been built up by archaeologists.

It is worth while looking at the problem itself historically— how did the recognition of a potential chronological content in archaeological evidence come about? The first step was the realisation that non-documented antiquity could in fact exist at all: that the whole of creation and the sum of human history was not in fact contained within the Biblical narrative. This was the repudiation of the theological model of the past, and once this and the mythological models had been disposed of, it was possible to glimpse the potential existence of societies which were absolutely non-literate and prehistoric. To contain this new apprehension of the human past, we have seen how the technological and evolutionary model was conceived in the nineteenth century, and the Three Ages, of Stone, Bronze and Iron, were invented to form a broad chronological framework.

But this at best provided a relative chronology on an all too generous basis—the mere fact that in any given locality it did look as though in the Old World stone was the first substance used for edge-tools, that in most areas this was followed by the use of copper and bronze for this purpose, and that iron was the last substance to be so employed until the Industrial Revolution. The problem of a more detailed chronology posed itself to nineteenth century archaeologists, and was met in more than one way. 'Archaeology has no dates of its own, gives no periods that can be expressed in chronological terms', said the Scottish antiquary, Joseph Anderson, twenty years after the publication of Darwin's *Origin of Species* had made a belief in an evolutionary process relatively respectable. Such a process Anderson does seem to have envisaged, but he could not conceive of archaeology as in any sort of alliance with history. But at least he was aware of the problems, and discussed them in his lecture of 1879, and we can see that in fact he had almost grasped the solution to this chronological impasse by what he said at the same time. He recognised that the archaeologist in Scotland, or anywhere else, would encounter two types of antiquities, those which by their numbers and character could be classed as indigenous to the regions of study, and those which were exotic to it, products of other communities near at hand or far away. But he did not envisage that such an association of local with imported objects could in fact give you the chronological relation between the communities producing the two classes of finds, nor that it would be possible for some imports to be the products of historically documented societies and so themselves related to an historical time-scale.

The fact that such situations could obtain in archaeological evidence had in fact been recognised by a contemporary of

Anderson's in Sweden, Oscar Montelius, who at the end of the last century laid the foundations of the method which we all use today in assessing the content and relationships of ancient cultures. He was concerned with constructing relative chronologies for North European prehistory at first, but eventually demonstrated how his system could be extended to involve the time-sequences of the Classical and of the Ancient Oriental worlds.

We can conveniently deal with relative chronology first, the arrangement of the products of non-historic societies into a time-relationship which may not have any dates, but which has a sequence—this is earlier than that, the other is later than both, and so on. Such sequences can be established by two basic sets of techniques; the comparison of the types of object themselves (forms and decoration of pots, types of bronze axe-blades, styles of flint-flaking), which is essentially the Montelian method, and on the other hand, the observation in the field which will assign objects, and the communities they represent, to their relative time-scale, in terms of their relationship in natural or artificial stratigraphy.

By the end of the nineteenth century the relation of archaeological material to stratigraphy was on the whole limited to the correlation of the earliest stone industries of north-west Europe with the framework of the geology of the Quaternary Period so far as that itself had been worked out. Stratigraphical information of the kind we now expect to be provided from excavations was virtually non-existent, because the techniques which could produce it had not been devised and elaborated. But on the other hand a great number of prehistoric objects had been found, and were available for study in museums and private collections: these were either single discoveries ('stray finds' to the archaeologist), groups of objects deliberately buried in antiquity for one reason or another ('hoards'), or groups of objects buried with the dead in graves ('grave-groups') which even the unscientific excavators of a past age usually managed to keep together in their original association. As this was the material available, the earlier systematisers such as Montelius had no option but to try to devise methods of extracting chronological information from it, if they were not to be wholly defeatist like Anderson.

We have already seen something of typology and comparison in Chapter II, and I hope appreciated that there is nothing more mysterious in an archaeologist deciding on the date of a bronze axe than someone who is no archaeologist deciding that the 1958 Cadillac is later than the 1905 Renault, not because it has a date printed on it, but because its design makes it necessary to place its building after, and not before, the Renault. In the same way we can look at a church and say that it was built in the twelfth century, with a new chancel in the fourteenth century, and a porch added in Victorian times, or recognise the difference between a Hepplewhite chair and one made in the reign of Henry VIII. So far, so good. Here we are dealing with things made by historically documented societies, and so we can give actual or approximate dates. With the bronze axe, however, the nineteenth century archaeologist could at best assign it to a nebulous 'Bronze Age' of uncertain antiquity.

Why then can we now place this axe in a much more secure position? The archaeologist's phraseology would be in terms of his technical jargon, but whatever he said would express the relative chronological position of the people who made axes of this sort in the general time-scale of the prehistoric and historical sequence of communities occupying the region in which the axe was found, and this would be the result of applying the principles of comparison, typology and association which we have already glanced at in the last chapter.

Montelius saw that, using the material available to him at the end of the nineteenth century in northern Europe, you could construct a relative chronology, region by region, into which the finds could be fitted. This chronology was partly based on the typological development of tools and weapons, checked by the occurrence of these in hoards or graves. Hoards are more tricky source-material than graves, for they can, for instance, contain scrap metal consisting of objects whose dates range over some centuries: just as with hoards of coins, you can normally only

PLATE IV. Selective excavation to tackle a specific set of problems—cuttings at Stonehenge, 1954.

date the time of deposition by the latest object in the find. When a relative chronology had been built up for one region—preferably a natural geographical area, rather than one within the bounds of modern political frontiers—it could be shown that certain objects, or certain modifications in type, could only be explained by contact with the technology of another area, and so the two could be brought into an approximately contemporary position. (This was the point so nearly grasped by Anderson in 1879 when he recognised that indigenous and exotic objects could be distinguished). For the time being we must leave Montelius and his methods at this point, though it is easy to see how in due course his method was extended to join up non-historical and historical time-scales.

But continuing with the methods of constructing relative time-scales, we must now consider how these can be devised by other means. The first is the relationship of the successive stages of human culture to naturally formed deposits, such as the gravel terraces along the courses of rivers produced by the processes of aggradation and cutting-back in response to variations in the flow of the water. Flint implements for instance may be found in such gravels, either sharp-edged, showing that they were incorporated soon after making and abandonment, or with the edges blunted by rolling with other stones in a gravel derived from elsewhere. The relationship between implements and gravel is clearly not the same in the two instances. If the formation of river-terraces can be related to other natural phenomena, such as changes in climate which will result in a partial thawing of the great ice-masses so as to increase water-flow, or changes in the sea level due to this or other means, the human industries can be related to major geological phases.

The relation between settlements and shore-lines can sometimes be very informative in this respect, especially when one is dealing with the material remains of communities whose economy was connected with waterside activities such as fishing or the gathering of shell-fish. In Scandinavia a sequence of changing pottery styles among such peoples early in the second millennium

B.C. can be neatly equated with the changes of sea-level of what is now the Baltic Sea. In the south-east of England, to take another example, there is evidence of human occupation on ground now covered by the sea at high-tide, so that there has been a rise in the sea-level (or a fall in the land, which amounts to the same thing) since that occupation. And not very far away, inland in the area of the Cambridgeshire Fens, there is evidence that there was an incursion of the sea, which left a thick deposit of clay containing the remains of minute marine organisms, at a time which geological and archaeological evidence agree in making contemporary with the subsidence of the Essex Coast. We have therefore a relative chronology established for the two regions together: if we could only relate the British phenomena to the similar changes in land and sea level in Scandinavia (which we cannot do in detail at the moment) we could extend our correlations across the North Sea.

In fact, if a tie-up can be made between local human events and widespread natural phenomena, an obvious method of linking chronologies in different regions presents itself. The French archaeologist, Claude Schaeffer, has recently tried to do precisely this for the chronology of Western Asia in the period from about 2500 B.C. to 1000 B.C., by identifying the results of earthquakes on a number of excavated sites. His thesis needs two assumptions—the first that earthquake shocks will be felt simultaneously, and inflict comparable damage, over a large area of the Near East, and the second that earthquake damage can be identified as such by the excavator. The first does not appear to recommend itself to seismologists and vulcanologists, who concern themselves with such problems, and with regard to the second, the question of the reliability of archaeological evidence as presented in excavation reports immediately arises, as in many instances Schaeffer infers earthquake destruction on a site on the evidence of his own reading of the data presented in someone else's report. It is an interesting example of the difficulties inherent in any such attempt to correlate natural and human phenomena.

The most rewarding set of techniques for such correlations has already been mentioned, the co-operation of the archaeologist with the palaeobotanist. So far as Northern Europe is concerned, a sound relative chronology applicable to large areas is now becoming available, as an increasing number of archaeological sites and objects are being related to the changes in natural vegetation detected by the varying proportions of pollen-grains in a stratified series of samples. We have already had a brief glance at this technique in Chapter II, and seen that it depends on certain factors—that the pollen-grains of the various plants are distinguishable one from another under the microscope; that the grains are surprisingly resistant to decay, and that their percentages in a given sample of soil will reflect the proportions of plants growing in the vicinity at the time of their deposition.

If there is no human interference in a region, plant cover (ranging from trees to the smallest forms) will reach what is called a botanical climax, which represents the maximum number of species which can exist within the limitations imposed by climate, soil, elevation and the competition of other plants for growing space. The main controlling factor here is the climate, and when successive deposits in peat-bogs or lake-beds were first examined by means of pollen analysis, it was soon seen that the trees in particular reflected a consistent series of changes in forest composition in northern Europe. These ranged from the arctic or sub-arctic conditions at the beginning of the final retreat of the ice-sheet, through improving conditions in which for instance the birch and then the pine could rise to the status of dominant forest trees, and so into conditions approximating to those of modern Temperate Europe north of the Alps, where the natural forest (if given a chance) would be one of the type which includes a mixture of oak, ash and elm.

These phases in vegetational history were at first equated with the climatic phases which had been deduced from this and other evidence, but before long it became more convenient for the palaeobotanists (or botanists studying plants in the past) to decide on a series of numbered zones, starting from Zone I, with its tundra conditions indicating the ice-sheet not so far away, and going on for eight or nine zones until we arrive at the one which includes the recent historic past and the present day. Once this had been done, in the Scandinavian countries, north Germany, Britain and Ireland, it was possible to regard this as a relative time-scale within which archaeological evidence could be set. This on the whole needed new excavations in which the archaeology could be tied in with the palaeobotany, but even old finds could be used on occasion. Objects found in peat-bogs, if not too well cleaned by the museum authorities, often contained tiny bits

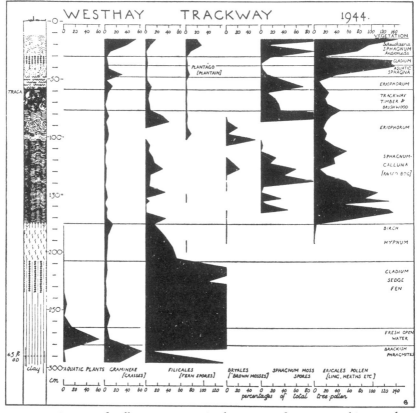

Fig. 6. Diagram of pollen percentages in the section of a Somersetshire peat-bog, showing changes in the local plant cover in relation to an artificial log causeway over the bog of about 500 B.C., at a depth of 60-70 cms.

of peat in their cracks or cavities, and since the standard pollen percentages were known for every stage, one could make a new pollen-analysis of the peat fragments, and from the statistics provided by this, suggest the place in the sequence where such a series of percentages would best fit.

As a result of this, we can now place individual sites or finds, and by extrapolation, whole archaeological assemblages, within certain pollen zones. All our earliest evidence of agricultural communities in Britain, for instance, are in these terms within Zone VIIB; the Roman Conquest took place in Zone VIII; the great extinct Irish Deer flourished on the grasslands of Zone II. This is all in terms of a relative chronology, it is true (though we shall see later that we are now getting absolute dates for the boundaries of the zones), but it is important in two ways. In the first, such facts as that of the appearance of agriculturalists in Zone VIIB for the first time do give us a position for our 'Neolithic' communities in the natural time-scale—a discovery of such evidence in VIIA would, in the present state of knowledge, be surprising in implying an earlier date (even if only a relative one) than that previously established.

But in the second place, the natural causes responsible for the changes in the type of botanical climax operate irrespective of human affairs over a large territory in Northern Europe, and so an archaeological find in Zone VIIB will be broadly contemporary with all other finds within this zone, whether they are in Britain or in Denmark. In other words, if you can assign a find to one of the botanical zones in Britain, you can then go on and equate it with other finds from the same natural zone in Ireland, or Scandinavia, or Holland, or Germany (or France, if we only knew what the French sequence was). You can say, for instance, that the famous lakeside settlement of hunting and fishing folk at Star Carr in Yorkshire is contemporary with such a site as that of Klosterlund in Denmark, because the pollen-analytical evidence shows them both to be late in Zone IV.

This process of constructing relative time-scales by pollen-analysis can be taken a stage further, so that a local sequence of structures otherwise undated can sometimes be set up. When a mound is thrown up onto the natural ground surface (for instance, a mound or barrow over a burial, or a bank thrown up from a ditch for defensive or boundary purposes), in effect it seals the piece of soil it covers and preserves the land-surface of the time. If this land-surface is of a type in which pollen will survive, it should be possible to see from a sample what the plant-proportions at the time of the making of the mound were, and to relate this either to a stratified sequence in the region, or at least to its position in relation to other local samples (the land-surfaces under a whole group of barrows, for instance). This has in fact been done with great success, notably in Holland, where in one recently studied barrow-cemetery it was possible to equate the pollen proportions from the old surfaces under the various barrows, which reflected changes in the woodland and artificial clearance areas in ancient times, with the stratigraphy of an adjacent peat-bog, so that the barrows could be arranged in a chronological series simply on the grounds of the type of vegetation growing at the same time of their construction. This was entirely in agreement with the archaeological evidence where it existed, but it enabled barrows with no direct archaeological evidence of date (except very broadly within the second millennium B.C.) to be fitted into the sequence. Similar work is being done in this country, especially in the New Forest and adjacent regions.

So far as the Old World is concerned, our knowledge of the vegetational sequence based on stratified deposits containing pollen is at present limited almost entirely to Northern Europe. The climatic changes which the plant-cover reflects must have affected large areas of Europe and Asia simultaneously, but so far we have little or no evidence which we can use from, for instance, the Mediterranean area. Recent excavations in Cyprus showed that the site at Enkomi had been repeatedly flooded over a period of years which could be dated around 1150 to 1000 B.C., and the excavator suggested that this might be related to widespread climatic deterioration perceptible elsewhere in Europe, but in the absence of the necessary data, this can only be regarded as a possibility. If the relative time-scale afforded by the successive climatic changes could be extended beyond the regions where it has already been worked out in detail, we could have a very valuable instrument of correlation.

The occurrence of archaeological material in naturally stratified deposits, then, can be used to arrange them in a relative sequence based on geology and palaeobotany. But there are other processes which will also provide stratification, which may be man-made, or the result of a combination of human and natural forces. One of the best-known examples of such stratification in prehistoric or early historic contexts, is that which occurs as a result of certain peculiar circumstances in many areas of Western Asia and in parts of Eastern Europe, resulting in the formation of artificial mounds composed of the accumulations of successive settlements one on top of another. Such sites, usually known in the Near East by the Arabic name of *tell*, have provided much of the knowledge on which our ancient oriental sequences have been built up.

Two main factors are involved in *tell* formation. In the first place, the communities occupying the site must have developed their agricultural techniques to a level which will permit a steady supply of farm commodities to the inhabitants of the village or town without the land exhaustion which under primitive conditions may cause agricultural settlements to move every few generations to new land. In much of prehistoric Europe this more primitive system was in force for many hundreds of years after the Ancient East had, for various reasons, been able to develop stable village and town communities.

The second factor is concerned with building materials. In early antiquity, as today, the main substance used in the Near East for the walls of houses, and of all but occasional monumental buildings such as temples, was clay or mud hardened by the sun. Walls of this kind were built up either by merely piling together the material, or making sun-dried bricks laid in mud-mortar, and the technique is very satisfactory provided the climate has summers hot enough to dry the mud quickly and efficiently, and winters without too much rain to soak the walls and reduce them to mud once again. Such buildings do not have a very long life, however, and when they need rebuilding the easiest thing to do is to knock down and flatten the ruinous walls, and build afresh on the foundation thus provided. The combination of these two factors—agriculture sufficiently advanced to enable a population to continue living in one spot, and a type of building which is renewed on the ruins of its predecessors—cause the accumulated layers of a *tell* to form as a stratified sequence. In exceptional circumstances (as for instance in the Indus Valley civilisation), kiln-baked bricks may be used, but the process is otherwise the same; stone rubble buildings too may become superimposed in a similar manner.

The process of accumulation is of course not so simple in fact as it is expressed in theory, and woe betide the excavator who thinks that it is! Save after sack and destruction, towns are rebuilt piecemeal and not wholesale; their sites are never level; domestic refuse dumps may exist sporadically; footings for walls may be dug from one occupation level down into the one beneath, so too may wells, rubbish-pits and graves. The working out of the various phases of occupation or temporary desertion, the detection of disturbances and rebuilding phases, the identification of the subtle soil changes which may indicate flood-laid silt or wind-blown sand—all these call for the utmost technical skill and judgement. It is no good trying to evade the issue, and assign finds to arbitrary 'levels' as in too many Oriental excavations even in the very recent past: Sir Mortimer Wheeler once drew a convincing diagram to show how it would be possible, in a hypothetical set of circumstances which might in fact easily occur, to find at the same depth beneath a datum-line, an object of 2500 B.C. (in an undisturbed stratum), another of the second century A.D. (later buildings on the edge of the *tell*, with foundations dug to the same level as the first find), and a modern coin (in a pit formed by pulling up a deep-rooted tree whose roots had gone down to the same depth as the other two finds).

This process of accumulated settlements or building levels takes

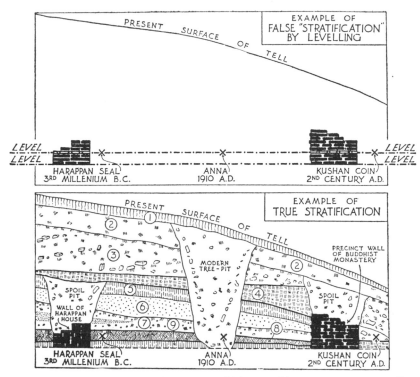

Fig. 7. Diagram to show how it would be possible to misinterpret a *tell* section if the natural stratification was not observed and recorded.

place, of course, in later times in many sites in Europe, notably the accumulations that have built up in Roman, medieval and more recent times in continuously-occupied sites, such as the City of London, for instance. Here Professor Grimes and his fellow-workers have had to unravel a fantastically complex series of deposits in order to work out the sequence of settlement.

Here, however, the excavators were dealing with historically documented phases of London's early history, and their task was to fit their material into a time-scale already established by historical means. It may often happen in a deeply stratified site, such as those we have just described in the Ancient East, that the upper settlement-phases are in fact those of people with an historical

record behind them—Islamic, Roman, Greek, Seleucid, Achae-
menid and so on. And in regions like Mesopotamia the historical record runs even further back, through the Babylonian
and Assyrian Empires, back to the kingdoms of Akkad and
Sumer, in the third millennium B.C. So these historically datable
settlements act as a point fixed in time by documentary sources,
and at least it can be said that any settlements before, say, the
earliest historical dynasties in Iraq, must date before about 3000
B.C. Similarly, if in northern Europe one finds a settlement underlying a Roman site, it must be earlier than the Roman occupation
of that region. It may be immediately before, or several centuries
earlier: how much earlier can only be perceived by the archaeological content of the earlier site, coupled with observations by
soil scientists in respect of the amount and character of natural
soil formation which may intervene between the two deposits.

It is not difficult to see then how a whole series of sequences in
individual *tells* was established, and how it was then possible to
equate, say, Phase Ten on one site with Phase Two on another
whose occupation started later, and so on, building up a comparative stratigraphy which could extend over large areas. Some
phases would fall within the range of history and could be given
absolute dates, others, earlier than this or without datable counter-
parts elsewhere, could be given a place in a sequence but hardly
anything more. Sometimes, however, a phase which was within
the historical sequence might contain objects imported from outside from peoples whose chronology was only relative, and immediately an absolute date could be transferred to the hitherto
undated sequence. This was in fact the way in which the first
dates were obtained for the Minoan civilisation of Crete, for
exported Minoan vases were found in datable contexts in Egypt;
similarly, dates in the sequence of the occupations on the island
of Lipari off the north coast of Sicily, where stratified deposits
really do resemble those of a *tell*, were obtained because imported
sherds of Mycenaean pottery were found in certain strata. Incidentally, the Mycenaean civilisation of Mainland Greece is
itself dated by Minoan chronology, which in turn depends on the

ancient history of Egypt! Similar to these accumulated deposits are those contained in natural caves, and some of these give some of the earliest sequences of human industries in direct stratigraphical relationship in Western Europe.

Stratified deposits may occur in burial sites, especially where a mound has been placed over the original burial. You may have, for instance, the primary burial in a grave, over which a mound had been heaped. Then, secondary burials may have been made into this mound, or even a second mound was sometimes made, covering the first, and containing burials of its own date, and then perhaps still later ones inserted afterwards. Such a state of affairs will give you the local sequence of burial rites, and of the types of objects buried with the dead.

In sites in which stratification of the *tell* type does not occur, it is nevertheless still possible to work out a sequence, sometimes almost in two dimensions only. Timber buildings are normally supported either by upright posts set in holes in the ground ('post-holes') or in bedding-trenches, or by upright timbers set on horizontal 'sleeper-beams' similarly set in a trench. The wood rots away, but the discoloured and softer soil of the filling of the post-hole or bedding-trench will remain to be detected by the excavator. 'Nothing is less perishable than a hole in the ground,' said a distinguished German excavator of the last century in this context, and by working out the successive structural changes in which posts were reset, or rotted ones replaced, or the ground-plan was altered, it is possible to see the sequence of events on the site even though there are no visible remains above ground-level. A Neolithic village in Germany could thus be shown to have been reoccupied six times after its initial founding, or again the story of the timber-built palace complex of the kings of Northumbria in the seventh century A.D. at Yeavering could be seen to fit in with the historical vicissitudes of the kingdom.

So then, much construction of time-scales can be made from the various forms of stratification and superimposition observed in the course of excavation, the validity of the sequences being in direct ratio to the competence of the excavators involved.

These sequences may be expressed in terms of relative chronology, perhaps as a numbered series, as in so many near Eastern sites, where one talks for instance of equating Tell Hassuna XI-XII with Tepe Gawra XII-XIX, Nuzi X-XII, Bakun A, Sialk III and Giyan Vc! But this archaeological shorthand for lining up a series of prehistoric settlements in several stratified sites has to be replaced by some other form of notation when deep stratified deposits do not occur. In most of Europe this is usually the case even if there are exceptional sites like Lipari, or stratified caves. Here one can talk of equating, for instance, a phase in the Lipari sequence with one in the cave of Arene Candide in Liguria, but other means had to be devised to interpret the archaeological material when this forced itself on the attention of scholars in the last century.

Of these scholars, we have already encountered Oscar Montelius, who with other contemporaries and many successors worked out the typological system whereby archaeological material even if not derived from controlled excavations could be arranged in local sequences, checked by the 'closed finds' provided by the occurrence of several types of tools, weapons, pots, ornaments and so on found together in graves or hoards. It was not long before local relative chronologies had been worked out for several areas—for the earlier Stone Age in France and Britain, for the Bronze and Iron Ages in Scandinavia and Germany, and so on. By the 1920s at least it was possible to consider these chronologies not only in isolation, but side by side, just like stratified *tells*. Instead of numbered strata, you had divisions within which consistent assemblages of archaeological types fitted: you said that Periods V and VI of the Montelius system for the Scandinavian and North German Bronze Age must in large part overlap with the Hallstatt B and C periods in the scheme by which Paul Reinecke had divided the south-west German Bronze and Iron Ages.

So far, so good, One could say that certain types of bronze tools, pots, and burial; forms of house and settlement and so on, which made up a 'period' or a 'phase' in each region of Europe,

Plate V. Brushwood and timber platform at a lake edge, part of a settlement of stone-using hunters and fishers about 7500 B.C., at Star Carr, Yorkshire.

were contemporary with another group made up of similar elements, but perhaps of quite different types. The tell-tale links which enabled the equation to be made were very often in the form of objects characteristic of Region B turning up in Region A (like the Minoan pots in Egypt). Now Montelius saw as his work developed that if this system of equations was extended gradually over most of Europe, there should be a point where one really did have a situation precisely like the Minoan pottery in Egypt—it would be possible by these means to connect non-literate, non-historic communities with those with an historical record which was expressed in terms of actual solar years. In other words, it should be possible to fix certain points in the regional, relative, time-scales which would have something of the validity of historical dates, and so produce the elements of an absolute chronology.

This is the theoretical basis for working out any absolute chronology for prehistoric or non-historic societies by means other than those obtained by certain scientific techniques which we will discuss in the last part of this chapter. But although the theory is relatively simple, it will be realised that the actual process is exceedingly complicated, and full of hazards and pitfalls. In Chapter V we shall see how the chronologies for the two great areas of ancient civilisation, Egypt and Mesopotamia, have themselves to be checked wherever possible, particularly in their earlier parts, and in Chapter IV we will consider the sort of grading between completely prehistoric and completely historic communities which affects the relationships between literate and non-literate societies in the ancient world. If one finds things which can be regarded as actual exports from a higher civilisation to barbarian peoples, these should, of course, give you a date for this trade. But the export in question may not be securely dated in the land of its origin—it may have been manufactured without much change for centuries. This is one of the complications which arise in connection with blue beads traded out from the eastern Mediterranean into prehistoric northern and western Europe around 1500 B.C. or rather later: the beads are certainly

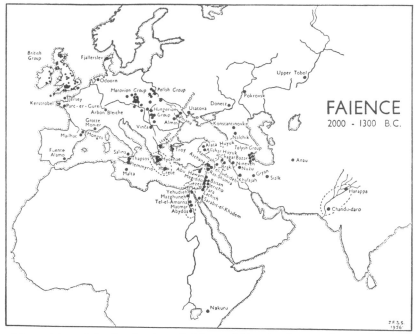

Fig. 8. Map of the distribution of objects of faience, of Oriental manufacture between about 2000 and 1300 B.C. and traded into prehistoric Europe.

of Oriental, and probably of Egyptian, manufacture, but it is difficult to fix them precisely to a really restricted date.

Sometimes the situation may appear to work in reverse, and barbarian objects will be imported into the civilised world of antiquity. Amber is such a substance, with its main sources of supply on the Jutland coast of Denmark, and traded down through continental Europe to the head of the Adriatic, and thence into the world of Mycenaean Greece around the time the blue beads were being traded in the opposite direction. Mycenaean traders were establishing themselves in the western Mediterranean too, and their characteristic painted pottery appears as datable imports in, for instance, the stratified sequence in Lipari already mentioned, where it gives absolute dates in the local time-scale.

With the establishment of classical Greek civilisation, and the development of colonies again in the western Mediterranean, there were opportunities for trade with the barbarians to the north and west, especially with the Celtic peoples. The Greeks and the Etruscans between them, from the sixth century B.C. onwards, carried on a brisk trade in wine with the Celts, and just as Chinese porcelain found its way to Western Europe with the tea trade of the seventeenth and eighteenth centuries A.D., so too did Greek pottery and bronze vessels get traded northwards, to provide fixed dating points in hill-forts in France or on the Danube, or in graves of chieftains in Burgundy, the Marne and the Rhineland. Later, of course, trade with the Roman Empire was to produce the same set of circumstances among the barbarians beyond the Imperial frontiers: Indian settlements in North America can similarly be dated when they first acquired imports from the European world within recent centuries.

In the last few years the question of prehistoric absolute chronology has been revolutionised by developments that are in fact by-products of atomic research. The method involves the basic property of radio-active substances, by which they slowly or rapidly break down by radio-active disintegration over a fixed period of time. Cosmic radiation in the upper atmosphere leads to the formation of a radio-active isotope of carbon with an atomic weight of fourteen, instead of the normal weight of twelve— hence C^{14} instead of C^{12} which is normal carbon. This Carbon 14 is a constituent of the carbon dioxide in the atmosphere, and is at a constant level. It is absorbed by plants, and therefore indirectly becomes a part of all animals. As soon as the plant or animal dies, no further Carbon 14 or radio-carbon is absorbed, and what is already incorporated will proceed to disintegrate in a normal radio-active manner, eventually becoming nitrogen. The rate of breakdown has been calculated in terms of what is technically known as the 'half-life', which is of the order of 5,568 years. This means that after this period of time, only half the original amount of C^{14} will be left, after about 11,400 years a quarter, and so on.

Now this means that if you can measure the ratio of C^{14} to

C^{12} in, say, a lump of charcoal from an archaeological site, you should be able to tell how far the radio-active carbon has disintegrated since the tree was cut down and used for fire-wood by the inhabitants of the site you are studying. In other words, you could get an absolute date which would be independent of any of the processes of making equations between non-historic and historic communities. This is precisely what is now being done in a number of laboratories; in America, where the technique was first developed, in Britain and in Ireland, in Scandinavia, Holland and Germany. Variant laboratory techniques are employed by different workers, and although there still remain many unexpected anomalies and difficulties to be overcome, dates are now being computed within a reasonably small margin of error, and with striking agreement between different samples examined by different laboratories.

The method can, of course, be checked against organic material of known age, and such control samples are in fact used. Recently the Cambridge laboratory, for instance, checked its radio-carbon apparatus by means of samples of timber from the galleys in Lake Nemi, known to have been made at the command of the Emperor Caligula between A.D. 37 and 41. The date obtained was A.D. 53 ± 95 years: this 'plus-or-minus' figure represents what is known in statistics as a single standard deviation, and does not indicate the range within which the actual date must lie, but that there is a two-to-one chance that the date lies between these limits. It indicates in fact the margin of error in counting the random radio-active disintegrations with a Geiger counter, which forms an essential part of the process.

Many other check samples have been used as controls, and remarkably close readings obtained. Since peat is basically vegetable matter containing C^{14}, it (or wood embedded in a stratified peat) gives an admirable opportunity of correlating the natural vegetation sequence already described, with an absolute time-scale, and an international programme is now being carried out to obtain radio-carbon dates for the junctions of the zones determined by the palaeobotanists. This is already producing most interesting results from many Northern European sites, and once the zones are dated, it follows of course that absolute dates on a rather coarse time-scale can be given to objects found stratified in peat deposits as soon as they can be assigned to a particular zone.

Radio-carbon readings can be made from various forms of organic matter surviving in archaeological contexts—wood and charcoal, antler and horn, shells, grain and even bones: recent work in Holland suggests that it may be possible to work from burnt bones, so that a cremated human body might, under suitable treatment, be made to yield the date of its burning. The method has great potentialities, though clearly there are technical difficulties yet to be overcome, and naturally the larger the number of samples examined, and the larger the number of determinations made on each sample, the nearer we will come to reliable dates of wide application.

A method of dating wooden objects (especially posts or beams) was developed in America in the course of the examination of native Indian sites where wood had been preserved owing to exceptionally dry conditions. This method (sometimes known as 'dendrochronology') depends on the fact that the annual growth-rings of timber are visible in cross-section, and that these reflect, in their relative thinness or thickness, the amount of moisture available to the growing tree. A run of exceptionally dry years will produce a series of abnormally thin rings, whereas heavy rainfall will similarly produce rings thicker than the average. By plotting these abnormalities in graph form, it has been possible, at least for the North American continent, to build up a series whereby beams or posts of unknown age can be fitted into the appropriate place. The inner rings of an ancient tree recently felled, and datable by counting from outside inwards, a year to a ring, may show a pattern of thicks and thins duplicated on the outer edge of another beam, which nearer its centre may have another set of anomalies, which can be picked up on yet another beam, and so on. By this means dates stretching back to about 1000 B.C. have been worked out in American contexts, and attempt have been made to make long-range connections with, for instance, northern Europe, but much more work remains to be done before convincing results can be demonstrated. That such connections are theoretically possible is suggested by the fact that the wet-and-dry variations as shown on curves plotted for tree-rings appear to be coincident with the curves plotted from the incidence of sun-spots in the eleven-year cycle which these exhibit. This would imply that there may be climatic variations based on this cycle which would operate all over the Northern Hemisphere, irrespective of, or overriding, local differences in annual rainfall and drought.

A somewhat similar phenomenon to the variations in the thickness in the annual growth-rings of trees is the presence in recent geological deposits of banded clays, in which the alternation of dark and light, and thick and thin, bands has been interpreted as the product of annual melt-water flowing from the edge of the retreating ice-sheet, and depositing silt in summer in the bottom of the lakes then forming. These bands, or varves, have been the subject of an elaborate investigation in Scandinavia, and to a less extent elsewhere, and an absolute chronology in solar years has been obtained for Sweden and Finland for a period going back to before 10000 B.C. But from the archaeologist's point of view there are many unsatisfactory features in the scheme, some of which are also felt by geologists. Above all, correlation between varved or banded clays, and archaeological sites, is always indirect. Certain geological facts can certainly be set within an approximate time-scale, and the work in North America has provided an independent chronological sequence for that continent. The whole system, of course, depends on the assumption that each band of silt represents a single year's deposition, and this assumption is itself under debate among geologists concerned with such problems.

Such then are some of the techniques by which archaeologists construct time-scales, in relative or in absolute terms. These time-scales are of course most needed in the phases of the past of mankind when there is no written record whatever. This may mean a context in time and space in which the communities under

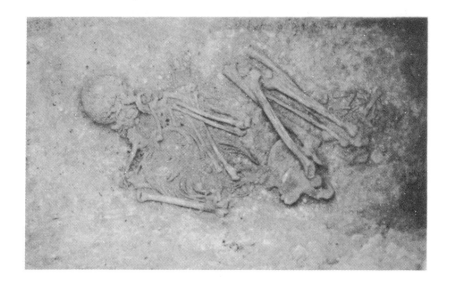

PLATE VI. Differing states of preservation of the human body: *above*, a skeleton preserved in chalky soil on Crichel Down, Dorset; *below*, stains in sandy soil with high phosphate content at Corrimony, Inverness-shire. Both about 1800 B.C.

consideration are wholly antecedent to all written history; on the other hand, we may be dealing with peoples living within comparatively recent times, and yet without a past documented in literary form. The techniques of archaeology, which include those devoted to the construction of time-scales, operate within the field of the prehistoric (or non-historic) past, and within that illuminated to a lesser or greater degree by documentary sources. We must now turn to consider these two fields, and to determine, as best we can, how the application of archaeological techniques differs in response to the presence or absence of a written record.

CHAPTER IV

ARCHAEOLOGY AND PREHISTORY

IN many people's minds there seems to be a confusion between the implications of the word 'archaeology' or 'archaeologist' and 'prehistory' or 'prehistorian'. Since it is only by archaeological techniques that the existence and nature of extinct societies without a written record can be detected and recovered, there tends to be a feeling that the archaeologist is concerned solely with prehistoric sites and their interpretation. This idea is one of recent growth, for less than a century ago archaeology would have been thought to embrace rather the material remains of the literate ancient world, classical archaeologists dealing with the products of the civilisations of Greece and Rome, and oriental archaeologists with those of the more ancient East. Such archaeology is, however, concerned with historically documented peoples, and we will discuss it in the next chapter. Here we have got to think about the application of archaeological techniques and concepts to non-literate societies in antiquity—in fact those usually loosely grouped as 'prehistoric'.

But 'prehistoric' is not such a simple word as it looks. Before history—yes, but what history? History in the region you happen to be talking about, or history in another area where the written record was in use much earlier or much later? The French, always logical in such matters, use *préhistorique* to mean just what it says—before history in the literal sense, before there was any history anywhere in the world. Written records of some kind go back nearly to 3000 B.C. in the Ancient East, so with their beginning there comes for the French the end of prehistory, whether it is in Mesopotamia or in the Orkneys, and presumably also if it is in Ohio or New Zealand.

Now this is just a bit too logical, and the word which has to be used to indicate subsequent non-literate periods, *protohistorique*, is not very satisfactory and too all-embracing if it is to include, for instance, the first agricultural communities in Europe (fourth millennium B.C.) and Eskimo societies immediately before European contacts brought them into history. On the other hand, the normal English usage of 'prehistoric', which is to denote peoples in antiquity up to the local arrival of literacy, at widely differing dates according to the region under consideration, conceals an important fact, and that is that after the first written history begins in the Ancient East we in the Old World have to deal with non-literate peoples living side by side with higher civilisations who are technically historic. The relationship between the two may be merely the accident of contemporaneity: the Early Dynastic Royal Tombs at Ur are roughly contemporary with the first agricultural settlements on the edge of the Swiss lakes, the date of one being computed from the earliest Oriental records, the other by the radio-carbon method described in Chapter III. But there were no contacts between the two worlds, whereas around 1500-1400 B.C. not only are their barbarian bronze-using communities in Central and North-Western Europe contemporary with Minoan and Mycenaean civilisation in the Eastern Mediterranean, but the two worlds were in this instance in contact through trade and exchange of goods such as amber, copper, tin and bronze. And then again, during the period of the Roman Empire there were large areas of the Old World inhabited by non-literate peoples beyond the Imperial frontiers, whether in Scotland and Scandinavia, or in India, who were nevertheless in touch with the civilisation of Rome by trade or other means.

In fact, so far as the Old World and especially Europe is concerned, we have to visualise a whole series of graded relationships between historic and prehistoric communities, in which with the development and spread of literacy (and therefore of a historical record), the relationships become closer and closer. In Europe, the end of 'real' prehistory (in the logical French sense) would come with the appearance of the first agricultural communities outside the Near East, and thereafter we have to deal with increasing contacts between the historic and the prehistoric world.

It has been suggested that we should re-define the general term 'prehistory' by making a major division between primary prehistory, 'the prehistory that precedes all history and underlies literate civilisations the world over', and secondary or marginal prehistory, represented by the peoples we have been considering, without a written record themselves but existing in closer or remoter relationship with communities which had. Primary prehistory can be studied only by the techniques of archaeology (in their widest sense, including the inter-disciplinary approach with the natural scientists), but secondary prehistory must take into account historical evidence and techniques as well as those of archaeology.

This is a useful concept so long as it does not involve a value judgement which would rate one or other division as having a superior relevance or significance in the study of the human past. What is important is to remember that because of the limitations of purely archaeological evidence, and of the inferences permissible from it, we are in a better position when we are studying societies which can be examined by more than one discipline— by history, philology and archaeology, for instance—than those for which archaeological techniques can alone be applied. We saw in Chapter I that one could make a useful distinction between text-free and text-aided archaeology, and this is really the same as the primary and secondary concept.

In fact, of course, so-called primary prehistory is not studied purely by archaeological means, but as we have just seen, archaeology combined with the disciplines of the natural sciences such as botany, zoology, geology and so forth. It is in fact just this co-operation between archaeologists and workers in other fields that has brought about the most significant advances in our knowledge in many aspects of prehistory. When one turns to text-aided archaeology, the task becomes more difficult (even if more rewarding) because not only has the close relationship with the natural sciences to be carried on, but a new inter-disciplinary

approach has now to be added, that which involves the archaeologist co-operating with the humanistic disciplines such as history
and philology as well. Really, of course, archaeologists working
in the field of prehistory have got to make the best of their
chances, and be prepared to utilise every ancillary discipline that
will help them to a fuller understanding of their material.

We have seen in the first chapter that the nature of archaeological evidence is such that it imposes strict limitations on the
deductions and inferences which we can hope to make from it.
We can find out much about ancient technology, a great deal
about all that is involved in the subsistence-pattern and economic
structure of the communities we study, but far less about their
social or political constitution, and very little about their religious
and spiritual lives.

We cannot, in fact, approach the extinct communities of the
prehistoric past as an anthropologist would turn to study a living
society today. Our thinking is controlled by the evidence which
has survived, which in its nature stresses the material aspects of the
people it now represents. We may be dealing with a society in
which myth and song, the dance and ceremonial rites, played an
overwhelmingly important part, yet to the prehistorian it may
be represented by a type of pottery and little else. What is important and significant to the archaeologists may have been
supremely irrelevant to the people originally responsible. We
have therefore to keep a watchful eye on our own presuppo-
sitions, and not, for instance, to equate a lack of well-made pottery
with an absolute poverty and degeneracy on the part of the inhabitants of the region which has disappointed the archaeologist in this respect. This may seem obvious, but terms such as
'poverty-stricken' have been applied in just such circumstances
by archaeologists, where the unfortunate groups of peoples
concerned have been even regarded as 'outcasts', driven from
one part of the country to the other 'before expanding, more
progressive, groups'—so called because they made better
pots!

This is an outstanding example of the pitfall into which

prehistorians can fall; to confuse their own estimate of what makes a satisfactory assemblage of objects of material culture, with what was satisfactory for the original owners, and with what can survive in terms of durability. We must remember too that the temper of our present age sets a high value on material culture, and on the increasing development of technological processes, and so an almost unconscious value-judgement is imported into the study of the past, in which technological innovation becomes a touchstone by which the worth of prehistoric societies is assessed. The fact that archaeological evidence is in large part the product of technology, and in large part too the incidental outcome of the subsistence-pattern of the peoples studied in the past, need not mean that the technological-evolutionary and the economic models of the prehistoric part have a superior validity, except in so far as they are among those best suited to deal with the type of evidence available. For communities in which we have evidence other than that derived from archaeology, alternative models can of course be used.

What then can the archaeologist working in the prehistoric field do with his available material? He has to try to arrange it in meaningful categories within the framework of one or other models of the past already discussed, and these categories should approximate to human realities in the long run. In other words, to arrange flint implements into groups according to weight or dimensions would be to form categories less related to the pre-sumed original intentions of their makers than to group them according to function—blades, scrapers, gravers and so on. The latter classification has to be made partly subjectively—'This looks as though it must have been used for cutting, so I'll call it a knife'—and partly by analogy—'This is the counterpart of the tools used by the Eskimo for scraping the fat off skins, so it is likely to be a skin-scraper'. Such interpretation can be checked by the knowledge available on the circumstances in which tools were made or objects used in the particular group under examina-tion, so that for instance weaving equipment will not be found as a part of the possessions of people who live in conditions in which neither animal or vegetable fibres are available for spinning or textile-making.

The prehistoric archaeologist, furthermore, is essentially dealing with anonymous peoples. He cannot assign his bronze swords which he has grouped in a typological relationship to a tribe or clan or nation. The settlement-site he excavates he can date fairly precisely, and the people who lived there made houses and tools and pots like others from similar settlements which can be plotted on a map. He has his site and the other similar sites, fixed in time, and he knows the geographical boundaries of the traditions in material equipment that they represent. But he cannot give a name to the authors of this common way of life which is reflected in his archaeological evidence. In these circumstances he is driven to considering not only how to classify his material, but how to name the classes into which it has been arranged.

The unit in which the prehistorian tries to work, in default of named groups of people, was defined thirty years ago by one of the founders of modern archaeology, the late Professor Gordon Childe. 'We find,' he wrote, 'certain types of remains—pots, implements, ornaments, burial rites, house forms—constantly recurring together. Such a complex of regularly associated traits we shall term a "cultural group" or just a "culture". We assume that such a complex is the material expression of what would today be called a "people". Only when the complex in question is regularly and exclusively associated with skeletal remains of a specific physical type would we venture to replace "people" by the term "race".' He went on to indicate that the geographical boundaries of such a culture could be determined by a study of the distribution in space of the constantly recurring traits already defined, and that if one found evidence of the transference of the associated elements of the culture outside its original geographical limits, one could assume a movement of peoples taking with them their characteristic traditions as embodied in their material equipment.

Such movements, as we know from historical examples, and from those happening in comparatively recent times among primitive peoples, can be of more than one kind. There may be a wholesale migration of families, clans or tribes such as those which took place among the Celtic peoples in the time of Caesar, or among the Germanic tribes at the time of the Saxon settlement of England, or those of North America within the past few centuries. Such a movement should show in the archaeological record a complete transference of household crafts, including that of pottery-making, which, by analogy with recent simple societies, is normally a hearthside activity of the women of the group until the use of the potters' wheel turns it into a business organised by the men. On the other hand, there may be folk movements comparable with those of the Vikings in early medieval times, or voyages of the type reflected in the tales of the Odyssey and the Argonauts, in which a predominantly or wholly masculine warrior-band is involved. If such raiding is followed up by settlement, the traits of material culture transmitted are likely to exclude pottery and similar crafts appropriate to the women, but to include types of weapons or ornaments brought from the original homeland of the raiders. We have too to reckon with what is portable and relatively unbreakable during the actual migration, and what is unsuitable for transport. Pottery made in the new territory can therefore represent a local variant on the types made in the original area of settlement, while portable tools and weapons can be brought and accurately copied after the journeying is over and the new settlement established.

Another archaeological concept which has to be used in prehistory is that of 'relations' between cultures as defined above. As Childe put it, whenever an agreement in material culture appeared in two otherwise dissimilar groups of traits, it 'must be assumed to denote some sort of relation, and, as such, to be a challenge to the prehistorian'. You may have two groups of people coexisting in time, but with diverse cultures, in which case some sort of interchange must have taken place between the two communities, or the correspondences may be in the form of survivals from an earlier culture, or the result of a mixture when new people come into areas already occupied by others of an alien tradition. And again, the agreements can be of different degrees

PLATE VII. The negative evidence for timber structures: *above*, post-holes of square tower within encircling palisade on top of a motte, 12th century A.D., at Abinger, Surrey; *below*, casts of decayed posts in rampart of immediately pre-Roman fortification, The Caburn, Sussex.

of precision: they can be generalised, such as two cultures both sharing the knowledge of agriculture, or of bronze-working, or they can be specific, as having identical brooches or arrow-heads.

Such 'relations' are certainly reflected in the phenomena constituting archaeological evidence, but their interpretation can be very tricky. The exchange of commodities between different groups of peoples for which one now uses the sophisticated word 'trade' can in fact take place in fantastically varied forms, and the mechanism by which any particular exchange took place between prehistoric communities must always be a matter of guess-work. We have to reckon on the one hand with all the varieties of what would today be thought of as a commercial exchange of some sort, in which some scale of comparable values is envisaged by both parties in the transaction, and on the other with the exchange of costly objects between chieftains such as obtained in the Homeric world and that of the Sagas. Nor can we expect to be able necessarily to perceive both sides of trade exchange in the archaeological record, since this is almost wholly composed of relatively imperishable substances, so that we cannot tell what hides and pelts may have been bartered for a flint hand-axe, or what corn or beer offered for a bronze sword. And still less tangible are important considerations like favour and goodwill, to be obtained on occasion by the judicious distribution of the appropriate trade objects.

An archaeological culture has to be defined in terms of its material content, but these have to be related to the dimensions in time and space. By the various means of dating outlined in Chapter III—stratigraphy, typological comparison, the evidence of imports from historically dated civilisations, correlation with the natural time-scale as provided by geology and botany, or by radio-carbon dating—the significant assemblage of material traits taken to define the culture has to be given its chronological limits so far as possible. Its spatial bounds can be approximately determined by plotting on a map all finds of the relevant archaeological types which constitute the culture. In theory a culture should be represented by all the aspects of the life of a community which would leave traces in surviving material objects, but this is an ideal seldom realised. The innumerable accidents of survival already mentioned conspire to make the preservation of even comparatively durable substances a matter of chance, and other accidental circumstances may also operate to render the record imperfect.

Unless the settlements or tombs of a prehistoric culture are built of sufficiently durable substances, or are of a monumental nature, their existence may be unrecognisable above ground. House-sites marked by no more than the pattern of discoloured soils which indicate the former presence of wooden structures can only be recovered by excavation, and excavation at a fair standard of competence. Until the late 1930s it had been supposed that the prehistoric farmers of southern England in the first few centuries B.C. managed in some curious way to live in deep pits, many of which had been found, containing archaeological material in their infilling. Subsequent excavations with superior technique showed that these 'pit-dwellings' were in fact storage and refuse holes, and that the farmsteads comprised various timber buildings as well as the farm-house itself, all indicated by post-holes which had been missed or not looked for in the earlier excavations. Had it not been for the more obvious pits, showing as dimples on the surface or clearly visible when accidentally dug through, the settlements of the culture would have remained virtually unknown.

In prehistory we are often in fact forced to construct a culture from evidence less complete than we would wish. For instance, many of the groupings which pass for cultures in the bronze-using peoples of Central and Western Europe in the second millennium B.C. are based on the contents of graves, supplemented by stray finds or hoards of bronze tools and weapons, and with practically no settlements as yet identified. Conversely, we may have settlements and practically no graves: the known graves of the first four centuries B.C. in Britain are miserably few compared with the settlements and forts of the same period.

To some extent, the archaeologist has to decide as he goes along

WEST KENNET LONG BARROW

ISOMETRIC VIEW FROM SOUTH-EAST

THE SOUTHERN CHAMBERS SHOWN AS IF CUT AT 3 FT ABOVE FLOOR LEVEL
AND PASSAGE CAP-STONES REMOVED

NORTH CHAMBERS

FACADE

WEST CHAMBER

SOUTH CHAMBER

FORECOURT & BLOCKING

BLOCKING STONES

FACADE

J.P. 1958

Fig. 9. A collective chambered tomb at West Kennet, Wiltshire.

whether or not a recurrent assemblage of elements of material culture is large and significant enough to be dignified by the name of a culture. The differences between many of the later stone-using agricultural groups in Europe around 2000 B.C. is simply one of pottery styles: what we know of the rest of the economy seems to exist in common among many such groups. Should we then call each regional variant of pottery a new culture? The problem faced me when I was trying to classify the comparable material in the British Isles not long ago: the so-called Neolithic or New Stone Age cultures as defined by the technological and the economic models of prehistory. I had to deal, for instance, with a number of stone-built chambered tombs, monumental and durable and so with a high survival-value and easily recognisable to the field-worker, but with hardly any settlement sites which could plausibly be attributed to the tomb-builders. And then again I found that a number of regional pottery styles were the products of groups of people who shared the same types of tools and so on in stone, flint, bone and antler.

With regard to the chambered tombs, I made something of a compromise. When there were practically only the tombs to deal with, with no knowledge of what traits of material culture might have been represented in objects buried with the dead, I had to fall back on stylistic comparisons between the architectural features of the tombs themselves, and their geographical distribution, to form them into what I called 'groups'. But when I had not only a group of tombs sharing common architectural features, but also a consistently recurring assemblage of material equipment buried as grave-goods, I felt justified in believing that I could talk of a culture. If settlements of these tomb-builders were to turn up, the assumption would be that the pottery, tools and weapons, ornaments and so on found in the settlement would repeat the assemblage found in the tombs.

The regional pottery styles accompanied by a common equipment in other substances seemed susceptible of explanation in a reasonably simple way. Chronological evidence such as stratigraphy showed that I was dealing with phenomena associated not with the first coming of Neolithic agriculturalists to Britain, but the end-product of a fairly long period of settlement and assimilation. The elements of material culture other than the pottery with its variant styles were almost all of the kind that one would associate with peoples whose economics were centred on the more ancient traditions of hunting and food-gathering rather than the relatively recently introduced crafts of agriculture and animal husbandry—in fact, with the people already inhabiting Britain when the newcomers arrived. Comparative evidence suggests that when a new culture is first implanted in a region, its earlier stages show a general similarity in elements of material culture such as pottery, spread widely over the whole region of settlement, but that as time goes on local traditions arise, with consequent regional variants and styles. So I decided that we had a generalised culture secondary in content (in that it derived from the original primary settlements, and had absorbed an increasing amount of the traditions of the indigenous inhabitants), in which the different pottery styles did not in themselves define separate cultures. Fortunately, there were other traits which could be used to make reasonable cultural groupings.

I give these examples to show the practical problems which the archaeologist has to face when working on his material. When the term 'culture' cannot be used, there are alternatives which have been employed, both in Europe and in the Near East, to denote recurrent grouping of material: of these 'assemblage' and 'industry' have been the most useful. The latter can particularly be used when one is dealing with stone tools, which for some of the earliest phases of human prehistory are virtually all the evidence available, apart from that provided by bones or plant remains indicating the environmental aspect. Indeed the study of man in the Pleistocene geological period (the Palaeolithic, or Old Stone Age of conventional nomenclature) presents peculiar difficulties of meaningful classification. Can one talk of 'cultures' in the same sense as one would when dealing with communities in the first or second millennium B.C., with their relatively full material equipment, when one is dealing with a number of stone tools incorporated in a river gravel, and of which many are of frankly unknown purpose? Here surely the word 'industry' is a safer classificatory term, unless the concept of an archaeological culture is so extended as to make it meaningless.

To sum up, the archaeologist working on prehistoric or non-literate societies in the past has to construct from the evidence of material culture a series of classifications which will approximate at their best to the grouping of human communities which can be perceived as tribes, clans and so forth among peoples with a literate historical record or surviving today. Around A.D. 500 a group of Germanic·tribes comprising peoples known as Angles, Saxons and Jutes, crossed the North Sea and settled in southern and eastern England: here we can talk of the Anglo-Saxon invasion, settlement, conquest or what you will, but we are at least dealing with people we know by name. But around 1700 B.C. there had been a similar settlement of much the same areas of Britain by people from approximately the same starting-points as the Anglo-Saxons, and for these people, known only from archaeological evidence instead of that of archaeology and history combined (as in the case of the Anglo-Saxons), we have no name. We do not know what language or languages they spoke, so tribal or per-sonal names are equally unknown. They did not touch the fringes of any literate societies, so we cannot even know what they were called by their more civilised contemporaries. We have to invent a conventional label for their 'culture', and from what to the archaeologist is the most significant and recurrent element in their material equipment—a well-made drinking cup of standardised form and ornament—we have produced the rather grotesque term 'Beaker Culture', and call the makers of the pots the 'Beaker People'.

To the historian, these curious labels which archaeologists stick on to their assemblages of material culture may seem at best clumsy, at worst ludicrous. It must be admitted, too, that there has been no consistency in the manner in which the names of cultures, or related groupings, have been devised. For the broadest divisions we inherit from the last century the Stone, Bronze and

Iron Ages; similarly, when at that time the Old Stone Age cultures (or industries?) were being recognised and classified, they were visualised within the terms of a geological model of the past, and given 'epochal' names like Acheulean or Cresswellian, on the analogy of Devonian or Permian epochs in geology. These classificatory labels survive, but for later prehistory we have a confusing variety of formations. We may denote a culture by the name of the site at which it was first identified, or best represented, so that we get Hassuna, Halaf and Ubaid cultures in Mesopotamia, or (following the geological analogue again) Badarian or Amratian in Egypt. In Europe we may compare names like the Maglemose, the Aunjetitz or the Hunsrück-Eifel cultures; in Britain the Windmill Hill or the Clyde-Carlingford cultures. Here the double names express the main geographical boundaries of the culture, rather than precisely located type-sites.

But this is (unfortunately) not the whole story. We have seen that the Beaker Culture in Britain is named from a characteristic piece of material equipment; on the Continent we have the Tumulus Bronze Culture, or the Urnfield Cultures, named from characteristic burial rites—under a barrow, or with the cremated bones enclosed in pots in a cemetery. Further complications arise when we use the old Stone-Bronze-Iron system, but with divisions which may be either chronological as well as 'cultural' in content (Montelius Period V, Reinecke Period D of the Bronze Age) or basically divided in terms of cultures of which only the initial dates are successive, but all of which finally co-exist, as in the British Iron Age A, B and C divisions.

In fact, archaeological nomenclature for the prehistoric past is far from satisfactory. It is inconsistent, and incorporates concepts deriving from more than one model of the past simultaneously. It is largely the result of a series of historical accidents, with classificatory systems devised to fit prevailing modes of interpretation—geological, technological, economic and so on. Among archaeologists it is a professional jargon, a short-hand method of expressing what may be complicated concepts of cultural assemblages. To the general reader it can only be confusing and often dismaying. In misunderstood form, it finds its way into non-technical works, so that mythical figures like 'Bronze Age Man' are created. The historian may count himself lucky that he can use valid names for his cultural groupings, and that the Norman Conquest of England does not have to be expressed as the invasion of the Motte Folk (and doubtless of Round-Arched Church People), and Edward the Confessor does not have to be concealed under the title of a Late Scratched-Ware chieftain.

I have discussed this question of the arrangement and nomenclature of archaeological evidence in prehistory at some length, since it is important to understand how the archaeologists' concepts of cultures, assemblages and so on compare with the concepts proper to historical studies. It may help, too, in the understanding of archaeological literature by those whose disciplines lie in other fields, or who come to the study for the first time. The main points to notice are that in the first place the prehistorian has to approach what were once living societies by means of their accidentally surviving and more durable possessions, then that as he is working in the non-literate past, he cannot relate what he finds to a linguistic group or to a people of known name, and so finally that he has to group his material and observed phenomena in meaningful categories which should have a real relation to the extinct communities they represent. For the consistent groupings of phenomena and objects which he calls cultures, he uses an admittedly imperfect and inconsistent nomenclature which serves him as a technical short-hand.

We may now return to the content of prehistory as perceived by the archaeological methods which constitute the only means of approach. We have seen that what we can perceive of the prehistoric past is governed by certain conditions of knowing, determined by the character of archaeological evidence itself. It will be instructive to look at some actual examples of recent archaeological research in terms of the information they have afforded of various aspects of prehistoric communities.

An inter-disciplinary approach, involving the co-operation of the archaeologists and the natural scientists, has been developed with conspicuous success in the northern European countries and in Britain, and its application to archaeological sites of the Late Glacial and the immediately post-glacial phases of climate has proved very illuminating. We are dealing, as we shall see, with communities with their subsistence-economies based on hunting, food-gathering and fishing, with a material equipment in stone, flint, bone and antler among the less perishable substances, and with a little surviving material at least in wood from among the large possible range of substances liable to decay. In archaeological terms the earlier sites are usually classed as Final Palaeolithic and fall within the Late Glacial phases of climate as determined by pollen-analysis; the later as Mesolithic, within the phases following the decisive retreat of the ice-sheet, determined as before. The dates of the particular sites we will consider range between around 11000 to 7000 B.C., and have been determined by radio-carbon tests.

The work depended in the first place on careful excavation, in which not only the archaeological material was observed and recorded, but it was studied in its natural context by palaeo-botanists and geologists. The earlier of the sites, Meiendorf and Stellmoor in north Germany, were in mud deposits which could be shown to be those forming at the edges of lakes in Late Glacial times, Zones I and III of the vegetational sequence determined by pollen analysis, with a climate and flora like that of the tundra today. The later site, at Star Carr in Yorkshire, was similarly on the shore of a vanished lake, in peat deposits which could be interpreted to show that the site was occupied towards the end of the formation of the Zone IV (Pre-boreal) phase. Radio-carbon dating places Zone I before 10000 B.C., Zone III soon after 9000 B.C., and the Star Carr site itself has been dated around 7500 B.C. Geology and pollen-analysis then have provided a relative chronology for the sites in the natural sequence of climatic and vegetational change, and the radio-carbon determinations have given fixed points in an absolute chronology.

As far as the technological level of the people responsible for these sites, their surviving material culture showed clearly enough that their basic material for edge-tools was flint, that they further worked in bone and antler and wood, and that at Star Carr they had cut down small birch trees with their rudimentary flint axe-blades. The typology of their tools related them both to the preceding Upper Palaeolithic cultures, and to contemporary and later Mesolithic cultures of Northern Europe.

In Chapter II, I have quoted the results of the investigation into the subsistence-economics of these people as an example of how zoologists can co-operate with the archaeologists on just such problems. The character of the settlements—with no trace of permanent huts or houses, but with every sign of a temporary lakeside camp—was that appropriate to hunters, and the debris of food-bones showed that at Meiendorf and Stellmoor the main quarry was the reindeer, whose natural habitat is just the tundra which the botanical evidence showed to be the natural environment. The age-groups of the bones when compared with the breeding-cycle of the reindeer showed that the camps were occupied in the summer. At Star Carr the changing climatic and vegetational conditions resulted in the main animals hunted being red deer, elk and roe deer, and here the age-grouping showed that we have to deal with a winter camp. Hunting equipment included bows and arrows and spears which, particularly at Star Carr, were furnished with serrated bone or antler points.

Up to this point then we have been able to deduce or infer a considerable amount about the basic character of the people represented by their temporary lakeside settlements: we can fix them in a relative and an absolute time-scale, and we can give a fair account of their mode of subsistence and the processes used to fashion their equipment in stone and other substances. The first two stages in Hawkes' scale of ascending difficulty in interpretation have been surmounted, and the evidence has permitted a considerable degree of legitimate inference. The small size of the brushwood platform at the edge of the Star Carr lake suggested that it could hardly have been occupied even seasonally by a group totalling more than three of four large 'undivided' families, and the evidence further suggested that the site had been used annually for about six years: the north German sites suggested similarly sized units of population, and recurrent returns to the same lakeside camping site. But nothing could be inferred of social organisation, except that, by analogy, the peoples concerned presumably had some sort of a social pattern comparable to surviving types among tribes whose economy is based on hunting today. But which type cannot be deduced: archaeological evidence fails at this point.

Beyond this stage, as we have seen, inference becomes even more difficult, but both from the north German and the Yorkshire site came evidence of non-utilitarian practices which can be vaguely classed as 'ritual' in intent. In the former sites, skeletons of young reindeer were found embedded in the lake mud, together with a large boulder: these were interpreted as sacrificial offerings, cast into the water and weighted down with stone. At Star Carr, a number of frontal pieces cut from the skulls of red deer were found, the antlers pared down to reduce weight, and the frontlets perforated as if for attachment. Here there are two alternative and plausible interpretations: that these were used as decoy masks in stalking deer, or that they were worn as a ritual cap in some ceremonies analogous to those carried out in similar disguise by Siberian shamans within recent times. The inevitable uncertainty of interpretation when we come to this aspect of prehistoric life runs through all archaeological evidence, as we shall see below.

The problem of ritual and belief among prehistoric peoples is posed in an acute form by a large number of monuments in western and northern Europe of the second millennium B.C., the stone-built chambered tombs, which in older classifications get included in a general group of 'megalithic monuments'. These structures are frequently on a scale, and of an architectural competence, which transcends the immediate needs of a simple family vault in which successive burials can be made over a period of time, and common traditions of planning and construction run through the whole group from the western Mediterranean to the British Isles and Scandinavia. Where the evidence is available, the objects deposited with the dead, or as offerings at the tomb, represent the local stone- or bronze-using cultures of the region in which the tombs happen to be: that is to say, that variants on a common tomb-type of monumental character were built by communities whose material culture did not share types in common. But the non-material concepts embodied in funeral ritual, as implied by the architectural setting of formalised and recurrent plan, do seem to have been shared.

The archaeological evidence comprises the tombs themselves, with their architectural features and techniques of construction; the burials in them, which under adequate circumstances of excavation can throw light on the manner of deposition and so the basic aspects of part of the funerary ritual, and the objects representing offerings made at the tomb during or after the burial ceremonies. The distribution of the main groups of tombs under consideration, from south Spain to the Portuguese coast, from Brittany to Orkney, implies that the traditions embodied in monumental form in the tombs were transmitted by people moving by sea. The burials, normally contained in a chamber approached by a passage or elaborated entrance, can be shown in most available instances to have been successive and collective; individuals were laid on the floor of the burial chamber, and as space became crowded and the corpses had rotted, the bones of the earlier burials were moved away or stacked at the sides of the chamber to allow room for the later occupants. So much we can deduce from the arrangement of the bones when carefully excavated and recorded, and we can add to this the information available in one or two instances when an anatomical examination of the bones has shown the presence of distinctive traits which can only have come about by the burials having been those of members of a related group or family.

The funeral rituals, it can be inferred, included the making of fires at the entrance of the tomb, and the placing here or elsewhere offerings such as pots which in some instances may have held food or drink, but in others were deposited as fragments after deliberate breaking. So that we have a picture of a common religious tradition stretching from the Mediterranean to the North Sea, expressed in archaeological form by elaborately planned and laboriously constructed stone tombs, in which a rite involving collective and successive, but not individual, burial was carried out, with certain accompanying ceremonies of which the material survival is that of fires and the durable portion of the offerings. It is at this point that we have to stop—from the evidence of archaeology we can infer very little more about what must have been a compelling and widespread religion in western Europe in the centuries around and following 2000 B.C.

It is perhaps permissible to make one further inference from the evidence, by using analogies from surviving religions. The distribution of Christian churches or Islamic mosques expresses in monumental form the range of certain religious concepts and ritual which demand architectural settings for the due performance of the relevant rites and liturgy, but the material culture of the worshippers and celebrants at church or mosque is that of the region in which they are built. The chambered tombs under discussion could then be interpreted on similar lines, as the architectural embodiments of a lost religion which included among its ritual requirements the building of monumental tombs to a prescribed formula, so that they would serve as the appropriate setting for rituals whose nature must remain unknown except in the broadest sense.

It is, in fact, funeral ritual which is likely to leave most traces in tangible archaeological form—what rites were celebrated in such structures as the stone or timber circles of the British Isles, at Avebury or at Stonehenge, must remain unknown, thanks to the very nature of archaeological evidence. Straining our inference to the limit, we can get as far as I have suggested above in the interpretation of the chambered tombs: beyond this we cannot go. We have been able to recover incidents in the ritual of many burials under barrows in the middle second millennium B.C., rituals which included the enclosing of the grave with temporary or permanent fences, and probably the exposing of the corpse before cremation, but what lay behind these fragmentary

pieces of evidence we cannot know, nor do we in any way understand how or why cremation or inhumation were favoured by
this or that community, or why there should be a change-over
from one rite to the other.

The question of social organisation and the pattern of society
must remain almost as obscure for most prehistoric periods and
cultures. Using the analogies provided by early historic and surviving primitive communities however we may infer from the
archaeological evidence the existence of certain basic types of
society, such as that which involves a graded class structure from
a king or chieftain through a noble class or a warrior aristocracy,
supported by peasant communities with an economy based
either on settled agriculture or pastoralism, or a combination of
the two.

Such a structure of society appears perceptible in the presence
of richly furnished 'chieftains' graves' over against a majority
with simpler and less costly funeral offerings, which occur at
more than one point in prehistoric cultures. In exaggerated form,
such burials can be classed as 'Royal Tombs', as those of the early
third millennium B.C. at Ur in Mesopotamia, a little later in South
Russia and Anatolia, and in the middle of the second millennium
B.C. in the Mycenaean Shaft-Graves. Less spectacular but akin are
burials of the same date as these last in central Europe and south-
western England. All these imply by their contents—fine weapons
and objects of a high standard of craftsmanship in precious metals
—the existence of a warrior class comparable to the heroes of
Homeric poetry or of Beowulf and the Sagas.

We know from literary sources that the Celtic-speaking
peoples, at the time they had become the subject of comment by
the classical world, had such a class structure, and when we turn
to their ancestors in the prehistoric past of the fifth century B.C.
in Germany and in France, we find the archaeological evidence
implying just such a society as the later Greek and Roman writers,
and the Celtic oral literature itself when finally committed to
writing in the early Middle Ages, do in fact describe. Even without the written evidence from the later centuries we would, from

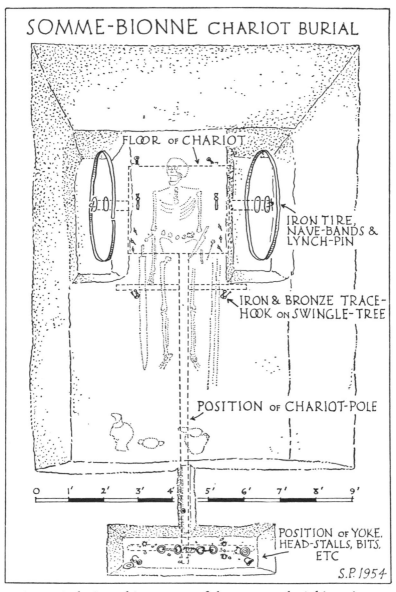

SOMME-BIONNE CHARIOT BURIAL

FLOOR of CHARIOT

IRON TIRE,
NAVE-BANDS &
LYNCH-PIN

IRON & BRONZE TRACE-
HOOK on SWINGLE-TREE

POSITION of CHARIOT-POLE

0 1' 2' 3' 4' 5' 6' 7' 8' 9'

POSITION of YOKE,
HEAD-STALLS, BITS,
ETC

S.P. 1954

Fig. 10. A chariot and its occupant of about 400 B.C. buried in a pit-grave
at Somme-Bionne, Marne, France. Of the chariot, the metal fittings alone
survive, as do the man's skeleton and his weapons and other objects including
an imported Greek cup painted about 420 B.C.

the archaeological evidence alone, infer just such a state of affairs. The burials of the Celtic nobility of the fifth century B.C. include several in which the dead warrior was buried fully equipped for battle in his war-chariot: not only for battle, but for the feast, with wine imported from the Mediterranean together with bronze flagons and Greek painted cups which allow us to date the graves containing them with unusual precision. The princess buried in the grave at Vix in the Côte-d'Or about 500 B.C. had included in her funeral offerings a vast bronze vessel of the highest standard of Greek workmanship, best to be interpreted as a present ratifying some concession granted by the Celtic rulers of the region to merchants or other emissaries from the Mediterranean world. For once in a purely archaeological context one glimpses what must have been a political act by a barbarian ruler with considerable bargaining power. Here, too, archaeologically represented, is one of the Celtic woman rulers known in later historical contexts in the persons of Boudicca and Cartimandua.

The activities of these politically and socially dominant elements in prehistoric society are again reflected in another outcome of the art of war, the defended hill-top fortresses wherein, in the inter-tribal warfare common to heroic societies at all times, refuge for people and cattle alike could be found. Such forts form a recurrent feature in the archaeology of western Europe in the second half of the first millennium B.C., their defences variously constructed in earthwork or stone, or one or the other combined with timber framing. From these forts we can infer the warfare that brought such structures into being (we may indeed see excellent analogies in the Maori hill-forts in New Zealand, still playing their part up to the eighteenth century), and furthermore see in their construction an expresion of some sort of social structure which could cause the concentration of labour to be brought to bear on such defensive works. In Anglo-Saxon society holders of unenfranchised land had obligatory services to the king which included the construction of forts, and the inference is surely permissible that some analogous obligation obtained in Celtic society, and that the building of hill-forts has left an indirect archaeological clue to its existence.

Behind this aristocratic display of power in warfare and patronage of fine craftsmanship, the peasant society is no less discernible in archaeological terms. Some of the most complete evidence comes from southern England, incorporated into the prehistoric Celtic world in the fifth century B.C., but with its agricultural character best displayed in sites of a couple of centuries later. Here we can see that scattered farmsteads rather than nucleated villages seem to have been the norm, with large circular farmhouses, granaries and drying-racks plausibly interpreted from the post-holes which preserve the plan of the wooden structures. Plough-agriculture was in force, and large surviving areas of ancient field-systems still survive even today; a cereal crop was grown and a computation from the provision for annual storage of the crop in pit-silos suggests an arable acreage of from about twenty acres to each farm. How the land was held, and what the legal status of the farmer may have been are the questions insoluble by archaeological means, even if we may sometimes guess back from the conditions obtaining in later Celtic societies.

It will have been seen that in certain instances it is possible by archaeological means to infer something of the social structure of a prehistoric society, though it must be emphasised that our reconstruction of the ancient Celtic pattern is heavily influenced by what we know, from literary sources, to have been the pattern in later times. We are in fact dealing with prehistory that is very near to history, and we are already using indirect historical evidence. In the next and last chapter we can go on and examine the way in which archaeological evidence can be used in the study of societies which have a written record of some sort. It is perhaps necessary to remark in passing that a written record which cannot be read does not transform the society which has achieved such a form of writing from a prehistoric into an historic one. We shall see in the next chapter how the Indus Valley script is still undeciphered, and how until it is, the civilisation that produced it as one of its manifestations has to be studied by the same purely archaeological means as we might study a Bronze Age village in Central Europe. The Minoan and Mycenaean cultures have, with the decipherment of the Linear B script as an early form of Greek, suddenly moved their status from prehistoric to partly historic cultures almost overnight!

CHAPTER V

ARCHAEOLOGY AND HISTORY

So far we have been dealing with the application of archaeological methods and techniques to the study of human societies in the past which are non-literate. It would be a mistake to think that there is a sharp dividing line between such societies and those with a knowledge of writing, and so potentially capable of producing a written record which could be considered historical in content. In fact, as we saw in the previous chapter, there are an infinite number of gradations in the societies usually grouped together as 'prehistoric', ranging from those existing wholly before any written record anywhere, to those co-existing side by side with fully literate cultures, and so to some extent half-historical themselves.

In the same way as we discussed the uses and limitations of the word 'prehistoric', we can profitably turn to consider the varying degrees in which a society can be called historic. We saw that if archaeological means alone are employed, we can only perceive anonymous peoples for whom jargon-names are invented by the prehistorian as a sort of professional shorthand to indicate this or that culture in non-historic antiquity. But as soon as we get non-literate societies living adjacent to civilisations with a tradition of literacy, we may at least find that we can give a name to a society known otherwise only from their archaeology, and sometimes we can add considerably more.

We can take examples of this from the Ancient East in the second millennium B.C., where several literate civilisations—in Egypt, Mesopotamia and Asia Minor, for instance—make reference in their records to peoples and places around the boundaries of their kingdoms who may otherwise only be represented by archaeological remains. Of course, the task of correlating the archaeological evidence with that derived from the documents is not an easy one, but at least the potentialities of identification do exist. And then again, Greek geographers and historians like Herodotus or Strabo give accounts of non-literate barbarian societies on the fringes of the Greek world from the fifth century B.C. onwards, so that we have for instance not only the name of the people who buried their chieftains in such richly furnished tombs in South Russia in the early centuries B.C.—the Scythians— but a lot of additional information on their social organisation and religious and funeral rites which can be added to that inferred from archaeological evidence, and indeed guide our inferences in the right direction.

Nearer home, both Greek and Roman writers give us infor- mation, as we have seen, about the people known to them as the Celts, at first in central Europe and later in more westerly and northern regions, including the British Isles. We know the names of tribes, of individuals, and of places within the Celtic world, and this can be set against the large body of evidence derived from archaeology, where the Celts lurk disguised as the La Tène Culture, or Iron Age A folk, or the Hill-Fort people, or what have you. With the Celts, too, the classical writers tell us much of interest about their customs, beliefs, clothing and so on. In fact (to go back to ideas we discussed in the first chapter), you can in some instances use an ethnic model for the past which contains the Celtic and allied people known to us from classical sources, and this is done when we talk about the Belgic culture of south- east England in the last century B.C. and the first century A.D., for we know that the archaeological material of that date in that region—fortifications, settlements, cemeteries, pottery, fine metal- work, coinage—can be attributed to the Belgae who, as Caesar tells us, came to southern England from north-east France before his time.

The instance of the Celts reminds us that we must not confuse an ignorance of writing in a society with a lack of literature, which, it must always be remembered, can exist in the form of an oral, word-of-mouth, tradition. Much of the early Irish traditional literature, in the form of tales and poems, though only committed to writing by scribes in the Middle Ages, harks back to the early centuries A.D. and to conditions which reflect an even older tradition, recognisably akin to that described for the Celtic world by the classical writers. This oral literature, then, although the products of a non-literate society, has come to be incorporated in the works comprising the literary heritage of a later society which did commit works of the imagination, and without direct utilitarian value, to the written page.

We can have, then, non-literate societies which nevertheless possess a considerable body of literature in the wider sense, composed, performed and preserved in accordance with an elaborate tradition of recital and memorising. This is the background of epic poetry the world over, but those societies whose oral literature was never, at some stage, written down, must remain voiceless and prehistoric to the student of the past. And we should take note of two other points in this discussion of the border-land between prehistory and history. The first is one we have already touched on at the end of Chapter IV—that if the archaeologist discovers by his techniques a literate civilisation, with inscriptions which survive on some durable substance, that civilisation has to remain prehistoric if the script in which the inscriptions are written cannot be read. The classic instance of such a civilisation is that which we would call in archaeological terms the Harappa Culture of the Indus Valley and adjacent regions—an elaborate and complex city-society, evidently literate since numerous inscriptions survive, but still anonymous and non-historic to us because they cannot be interpreted. A few years ago a second example would have been quoted, the Minoan and Mycenaean script known as Linear Script B. 'Minoan' and 'Mycenaean' are not ancient names of peoples, but archaeological inventions to denote cultures which if you used the technological-evolutionary model of the past would be classed as Middle and Late Bronze Age in the Aegean area. Until it was discovered to be an early form of Greek, the fact that the inscribed tablets in the Linear B script existed could not in themselves tell us anything of the linguistic affiliations of their writers, nor, of course, reveal their subject-matter. With their decipherment, the later phases of the Minoan and Mycenaean cultures move from complete prehistory into a sort of history.

The second point to be remembered about writing in early civilisations is that it could be, and often was, used for restricted purposes only, and not, as in a modern civilisation, for recording anything and everything which can be put into words. This restricted use of writing has been called conditional literacy, and seems in fact to have been the background against which the Mycenaean writing just referred to must be set. Here the tablets all seem to be of the nature of office memoranda arising out of a very efficient bureaucratic organisation for running royal estates or larger units, just as the earliest written documents in Sumer are largely concerned with temple accounts. Such an arrangement, with writing a technique known only to a few scribes, may well result in there being a language and a script which is 'official' and is used only for official business purposes. There is, unfortunately, little hope that we shall find fragments of a pre-Homeric Odyssey written in Linear B by a Mycenaean counting-house clerk. The literature of a people may well remain as an oral tradition side by side with conditional literacy for a restricted purpose. Another comparable example of conditional literacy can be found in the Celtic world, in Roman Britain. Here there were two languages, Celtic and Latin, and one script, the Roman alphabet introduced with the Latin language. In consequence, one has a situation where the only language of writing was Latin— 'it would not occur to anyone to write in British, nor would they know how to do so', says Professor Jackson, commenting on this point. 'One tends to forget,' he goes on, 'that to write down in an alphabet the sounds of a speech (even though it is one's own) which one has never been taught to write is a very considerable intellectual feat'. So once again, for formal and business occasions when writing was needed, a language and a script was used which in this instance had nothing to do with the vernacular literature transmitted orally.

This may all seem rather off the point, but it is in fact very important to appreciate the long range of gradations stretching from absolute non-literacy (and so complete prehistory) up to a complete and conscious written record in the full historical sense. When we come to consider the application of archaeological techniques to historically documented societies, it is with societies at every stage of literacy that we have to deal, not only those which are obviously 'historical'.

It is in fact for the study of those societies with an imperfect literate record that archaeological techniques have the greatest value, for they can amplify the scanty written sources and indeed, in countries where documents were written on relatively durable substances, such as baked clay, archaeology can add to the historical record by recovering additional source-material in circumstances of controlled excavation. The basic historical documents of the Ancient East were all discovered by archaeological techniques of varying standards, and even where more perishable materials were used, such as papyrus or parchment, these can again be recovered by the archaeologist in exceptional circumstances, as in Egypt.

By archaeological techniques then, written documents in durable substances, (notably clay, used extensively in the Near East, and again for the Mycenaean Linear B tablets just mentioned) can be brought to light, and so supply the philologists and historians with the essential sources for their own studies. From such written documents, if they are of the type which contain actual historical information in the form of lists of rulers of an area with the years of their reigns, or with references to astronomical phenomena (such as eclipses), it should be possible to reconstruct the ancient calendar of the people in question, and from this to make an absolute chronology. If one is dealing with societies at a degree of civilisation in which contacts with neighbouring communities involve treaty relationships or diplomatic correspondence, than a correlation between the chronologies of the two states becomes possible, as when Tutankhamen's widow sought a Hittite prince as husband, and wrote to his father to this affect.

Archaeology operating in historically documented societies has then the great advantage of having at least the broad outlines of the chronology concerned already worked out by non-archaeological means, even if these means are closely connected with those of archaeology. Further, there will be an outline at least of the historical events considered important to the contemporary chroniclers—victories and defeats, colonial expansion, trade and conquest. The adoption of the war-chariot by the Egyptian High Command, which could be perceived in part from purely archaeological evidence, takes its place in the historical setting when we know of the campaigns in the Levant during which the Egyptians met this engine of war for the first time, operated by their enemies, and thereafter used it themselves. The archaeological evidence for the structural phases of Hadrian's Wall becomes significant only when related to our knowledge of the events within the Roman Province of Britain; a similar series of building, alteration, damage and reconstruction might also be inferred from archaeological evidence for a native hill-fort, but could not be given an historical content owing to the lack of a framework of knowledge.

The existence of such a framework of knowledge enabled the development of archaeology within certain historical fields— Roman Britain is a good example—to be more rapid than that in a prehistoric context, because it was possible to envisage problems that archaeological evidence might solve, and to apply the question-and-answer process to them. With a basic historical background, it was possible to formulate an approach impossible to the prehistorian until he, by archaeological means themselves, had constructed a framework within which he could then see his problems, and could pose meaningful questions to be resolved by further archaeological investigation.

The main fields within which archaeological techniques have been applied to historically documented societies are three. The

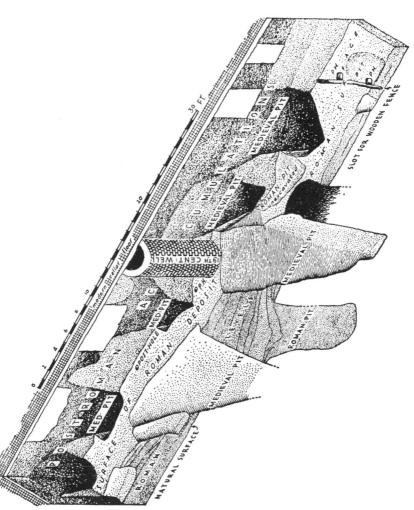

Fig. 11. The complications of stratigraphy in a long-occupied historical site: an axonometric diagram of Roman and medieval features in the City of London excavations.

first, and to some extent the most spectacular, is that of the Ancient Orient, the second, and longest established, is the classical world of Greece and Rome, and the last, and a comparatively latecomer into the discipline, is the post-Roman and medieval period in Western Europe. In all, as we shall see, the archaeologists' techniques can be applied in many profitable directions, but in all there are peculiar problems arising partly from the nature of the material, and partly from the historical development of studies within these fields.

In the first place, in the spheres of classical and oriental archaeology especially, the approach and the performance has been bedevilled by a preoccupation with the acquisition of works of art and their subsequent study along specialised lines. It must be remembered that classical archaeology in a rudimentary form has firm roots in the Renaissance, when sculpture in particular was sought for in an admitted and understandable spirit of aesthetic adventure. By the eighteenth century, the study of the classical past had arrived at a curious position which it was to maintain almost until yesterday, wherein the Greeks and Romans were the Great Exemplars, to be studied as patterns of conduct in private and public life, literature and the arts. The classical world had set standards and established canons of validity and applicability to the moderns, and its study had in fact a very practical aspect, since by it one could learn to conduct oneself with propriety, to acquire a correct taste in architecture and the visual arts, to know the rules of verse and prose and rhetoric, and to perceive, by analogy, the principles of just government and policy. In a word, the classical past was seen in terms of a moral and ethical model.

Classical archaeology thus inevitably began by being art history. Architecture, sculpture and painted vases were fit subject-matter for the student in this field, with numismatics and epigraphy by their side. With this concentration on works of art went (as we have already seen), the formation of collections both private and public in which the objects were rated solely in aesthetic terms, and so as a result the most terrible depredations took place on classical sites in order to produce objects of beauty without regard to their context or stratigraphy. Similar forces operated later in the oriental field, so that excavations were promoted by museums primarily for the purpose of obtaining spectacular exhibits rather than historical information in which the works of art could take their natural place.

To make these strictures is not, of course, to belittle the value of aesthetic experience—the discovery of a work of art is one of the greatest rewards that can come an archaeologist's way, but his work should not be directed solely to this end, nor is it today. We must remember the changing temper of thought which no longer regards the ancient world as a storehouse to be pillaged for works of art which will serve as models to mould the taste of our own sculptors and painters into the right tradition. We formulate questions about the classical or the Oriental past in terms inconceivable to the students of ancient history or the classical archaeologists of a generation or two ago, and many of these questions can be best answered by archaeological means, or these means in co-operation with historical disciplines. We no longer use the moral and ethical model of the Greek and Roman past, nor one exclusively conceived in terms of aesthetics, but seek to include the art and architecture of the societies concerned within the wider field of the total products of human endeavour which devised the society which we are engaged in studying.

So far as the practical application of archaeological techniques to such historically documented societies as those of Sumer or Egypt, Greece or Rome, is concerned, it is clear that the standards of field-work and excavation must be no lower in these fields than in those of, for instance, European prehistory. Much of the development and refinement of excavation technique has, as we have seen, taken place as the result of circumstances in which the material culture of the peoples studied has been scanty and difficult of recovery, so that every scrap of evidence has to be wrested from the site by one ingenious process after another. On classical and Oriental sites, on the other hand, the surviving structures and objects representing the material culture of the inhabitants of a village or town, or deposited with the dead in cemeteries, are likely to be almost overwhelmingly abundant and conspicuous, so that a rough-and-ready idea of, for instance, the stratigraphic sequence in a site could be obtained without the exercise of much archaeological expertise. This has in the past been used as an excuse for incompetent excavation, but is not an argument which will bear a moment's critical examination. The application of excavation techniques at a high level of competence has shown how much more can be extracted from a site by such means, and we shall see some examples of this later on.

What is needed in the application of archaeological techniques to historical societies is in fact all the expertise devised for the examination of non-literate, prehistoric, peoples (including the co-operation with the natural scientists), further combined with a co-operation between the archaeologist and those working in the humanistic disciplines involved in, for instance, philology and history. In this sense, the archaeologist's task is harder when he works in the historical field than when he is dealing with non-historical antiquity. In the latter sphere he has to understand the disciplines involved in the studies by geologists, botanists, zoologists and so on which with his own archaeological evidence can build up the ecological and environmental background, but the nature of his evidence sets a limit to the investigation he can make into the society he is studying. The additional sources which can be classed as historical in the wider sense, however, extend the potentialities of knowledge at the same time as they demand a further inter-disciplinary comprehension by the archaeologist.

With such a co-operative approach, the application of archaeological techniques to historical societies can in fact amplify the strictly literary record in many directions. In the first place, it must be remembered that many significant and important human activities never get recorded in written form until we reach the self-conscious and fully literate societies of the modern world, but that these activities are just those which can in many instances be perceived by archaeological means. Agriculture and husbandry, the preparation of food and drink, the craftsmanship of the carpenter, the wheelwright and the mason, the technological processes employed by potters and metal-workers—all these, in pre-industrial societies, were traditional and unwritten skills handed on within the family, or from master to apprentice. But the products of these crafts are after all the subject-matter of archaeologists, and it is by archaeological means that we can recover some of the ancient technology which itself laid the foundations of experimental and speculative science no less than those of industrial processes.

We may notice in passing that the study of such aspects of ancient societies seems important to us today, since the temper of the age is a technological one, and we tend to use models of the past which stress the technological and economic aspects, believing that by their use we may get a more 'true' picture of antiquity. When classical archaeology (and to some extent that of the Ancient East) was first developing as a discipline, we have seen that the model of the past employed was a moral, ethical and aesthetic one, so that out of the total of surviving material culture the architectural and artistic objects were selected as significant subjects of study. In fact, the art-historical disciplines which developed out of this approach are entirely analogous to those of archaeology, and the art-historian's attribution of a painted Greek cup to a particular painter uses a system of reasoning on precisely the same lines as that used by the prehistorian when he attributes a sword-scabbard of the second or third century B.C. to a Swiss rather than to a south German workshop (though found in the latter area), or when he assigns a Palaeolithic industry in stone and bone to Magdalenian I rather than to Magdalenian VI. In the same way, and in a later field of historical study, the architectural historian who works out the building sequence in Canterbury Cathedral or the Tower of London would use the same basic techniques as the archaeologist making a similar study of Stonehenge or Maiden Castle.

The archaeological contribution to historical studies can therefore be of some significance when we are concerned with ancient technology, whether in the simpler forms of fabrication or construction, or in those manifestations of technology which are also works of art. It can also illuminate the relationship of the community to its natural environment, and its degree of control over nature as expressed in the domestication of animals, cultivation of cereal and other vegetable foods, or the production of fibres for textiles from natural sources. It can again throw light on aspects of trade not necessarily recorded in any documentary sources, by examining and identifying the materials used in building or for the manufacture of artefacts in use by the community under review. By applying the techniques of controlled excavation, it can sometimes supplement the existing written record by providing additional documents, or act as a check on the typological arrangements of the art-historians by finding stylistically significant pieces in dated contexts. Conversely, of course, a well-established typological series, like that of painted Greek vases, can themselves be used by archaeologists as dating material when characteristic sherds occur in stratigraphical contexts, as we have seen in Chapter III. The two techniques—stylistic analysis and the principles of archaeological closed finds—are complementary and interdependent.

Before we proceed to discuss some actual examples of the use of archaeological techniques in such contexts, we must for a moment go back to the sort of questions about nomenclature that we encountered in Chapter IV, but now in connection with archaeological names for historical situations. In the Near East, for instance, a curious double system of classification has come about, as the result of using two different models of the past for the same evidence. On the one hand, we have historically attested civilisations such as those of the Hittites, the Egyptians or the Sumerians, each with a complex material culture varying according to the civilisation itself, and again within that civilisation in relation to its internal development. If then we use an historical model, as is often done, we can talk about Hittite bronze tools or pottery of the kingdom of Solomon. But alternatively, if we use the technological-evolutionary model, based on the Three Ages system of the nineteenth-century Danish prehistorians, the tools come into the Anatolian Middle or Late Bronze Age, and the

PLATE VIII. Dating by imported objects: *above*, Greek drinking-cup painted between 530 and 520 B.C. from the 'Princess' grave at Vix, Cote-d'Or, France; *below*, fragments of pottery from the nearby hill-top fortification of Mont Lassois, 1-4 native wares, 5 and 6 fragments of Greek vases of the sixth century B.C.

pottery into Israelite Iron Age I. This is a situation which can cause some confusion, and it seems a pity that we should have to use the technological model, which is at best an expedient for classifying the material culture of non-literate societies, when we could assign some of the material at least to actual peoples. On the other hand it must be remembered that not all the peoples concerned are in fact historically documented, so some concept for describing people contemporary with and adjacent to the Hittite New Kingdom, for instance, but themselves non-historical, is needed.

Among the disciplines with which the archaeologist working on historical peoples has to deal, is that of philology or linguistics: the languages spoken by the various cultural groups in antiquity. In literate societies the language or languages used are of course embodied in the written documents, which in addition to any historical or literary value they may have, are also valuable from the purely linguistic viewpoint. But there are interesting problems on the borderlands of history and prehistory where linguistics are involved, but not all the societies we are studying are literate, so that the archaeologist has an important part to play.

We saw earlier on that by the time the existence of a Celtic language in Central and Western Europe is attested by the classical writers, the archaeological evidence shows that the peoples speaking this tongue had been long established in their homeland east of the Rhine. The general principle one goes on (which sounds simple, but is really very complicated) is that if you have a language historically attested in a region at a certain date in the past, and you can equate this language with a 'culture' in the archaeological sense, then if you work backwards you can assume that the same language (or its earlier form) was spoken so long as the archaeological culture-sequence is unbroken. If in stratified sites you suddenly find, as you work backwards in this way, that there is a complete change in material culture, perhaps accompanied by evidence that an older culture has been forcibly changed by new-comers with, for instance, the burning of the earlier settlements, then you can reasonably assume that this break in the continuity of the archaeological material might be equated with a linguistic change. As I said, this sounds fairly easy, but the situation is in fact full of difficulties. On the other hand, there are ways and means of making one's reasoning less fallacious than it might be on purely archaeological evidence.

The Celtic languages belong to a great linguistic family of related dialects and languages which for a century or so have been recognised as the Indo-European group, the name indicating that the geographical range of languages in the group do extend, or has extended in the past, from India in the east to Europe in the west. The recovery by archaeological means of documents in languages used in the Hittite Kingdom showed that some of these were in fact members of the Indo-European group, and also provided the earliest dated specimens of such a language, with a date not long after 2000 B.C. To the group also belong Sanskrit in India, Greek, Latin, and as we have seen, the Celtic languages as well, and other tongues mainly known only from relatively late documents or modern survivals.

The linguistic relationships between these languages made it necessary for the philologists to assume that they all derived either from a single ancestral language, or at least a group of closely related dialects spoken by groups of people in close proximity one to another. Further than this, certain words which were shared in common in languages scattered far and wide within the Indo-European language group indicated that they must have been part of the ancestral common tongue, and when some of these represented elements of material culture, it was possible for archaeologists and linguists to join their techniques in an effort to solve a common problem. Here again, the situation is not so simple a one as it sounds when stated briefly, but the sort of significant features noted were the lack of a common word for 'iron', though one existed for 'copper' or 'bronze', or again a word in common for 'horse', and for various parts of a wheeled cart (the hub and axle of the wheel, the wheel itself, the yoke for harnessing the draught animals), but, interestingly enough, diverse words for 'chariot'. Other correspondences relating to environmental factors affecting the original genesis of common Indo-European included words for the birch-tree and a large river-fish, probably the salmon, but no common word for 'sea'.

It was possible, in fact, for the linguists to sketch out a tentative outline of a certain type of material culture, with certain limitations as to likely geographical areas—somewhere where the horse could be known, for instance, with large rivers, but not on the seacoast and so on. And when evidence appeared that the Indo-European languages spoken in the Hittite Kingdom must have split off from the parent stem round about 2000 B.C., and probably before that, the archaeologists were set a problem with certain controlling factors of chronology, geography, and type of material culture. Let me say at once that the problem of the original homeland of the Indo-European languages has not been settled, and that it is likely that, stated in such simple terms as this, the problem of directly correlating language and material culture in the pre-literate antiquity of the late third millennium B.C. is in fact insoluble. Furthermore, complications have been added as a result of the reading of the Linear B script in the Aegean area as an early form of Greek, and the difficulty in deciding whether what seem to be reflections of a complex form of society and land-tenure embodied in words of common Indo-European parentage set down in the tablets are to be taken as denoting elements to be sought for in the original Indo-European communities, or whether they are concepts taken from the higher civilisations of broadly Oriental derivation, encountered by the first Greeks in the Aegean world, and denoted by words already existing in their own language.

At all events, the collaboration between linguists and archaeologists on these problems is full of promise. Archaeology and history together show, for instance, that the horse as a draught animal was a relatively late introduction into the ancient Oriental world of the Near Eastern civilisations, and must have been an original denizen of the steppe lands. Similarly, while wheeled carts can be traced archaeologically well into the third millennium B.C., the war-chariot was a late development around

1500 B.C. So the original Indo-Europeans are likely to have lived in areas on or adjacent to grazing ground for wild horses, outside the area of the urban civilisations in western Asia, and to have adopted the war-chariot, in common with other peoples speaking quite different languages, after the time of their dispersal. Somewhere between the Carpathians and the South Russian plains some of the early metal-using cultures known to the archaeologist ought, on all reasonable probabilities, to have been those of people who spoke early Indo-European dialects. Somewhere further west, in central Europe, the ancestors of the historical Celts await identification among the archaeological cultures of the early second millenium B.C. And somewhere in Pakistan there should some day be found archaeological evidence for the Sanskrit-speaking Aryans who brought their language to the Indian sub-continent in the second half of the second millennium B.C. The problems are fascinating, and can only be approached by the inter-disciplinary methods of historians, linguists and archaeologists working in close co-operation.

When we turn to the earliest historical civilisations of the Near East we enter a field in which the archaeologist has made some of his most notable contributions, and in which the literary evidence on its own would for many centuries present a very sketchy picture of the life and achievements of, for instance, the earlier dynasties of Sumer or of Egypt. Here in fact archaeological evidence is of such importance that it is often taken for granted that our knowledge of these early civilisations is based wholly on such data. In so far as the recovery of material is concerned, of course, the archaeological techniques of excavation have been of prime importance both for obtaining a full picture of the material culture of the civilisations involved and, as we have seen, for similarly providing for the linguist and historian the written documents themselves. By wholly archaeological means, too, the stratigraphical (and so chronological) relationship between the earliest literate societies and those without writing has been established in numerous instances, so that viewed from the archaeological standpoint alone one appears to perceive a continuous sequence of technological progress from the earliest village settlements to the first urban centres, following virtually identical lines in (for instance) Egypt and in Mesopotamia. In such a sequence writing appears as an incidental technological innovation resulting from the necessity of having a system of notation within an increasingly complex society by which permanent records could be kept of such things as temple accounts.

In fact, if you use the technological-evolutionary model you obtain the familiar stone-copper-bronze sequence for tools and weapons, or if you use the economic model, you then contain this within another sequence, from hunting and food-gathering communities, through those with settled agriculture and villages, into the complex 'Bronze Age' urban economies which in turn become 'Iron Age' communities of the same type. Within the terms of the economic model, Gordon Childe, using a concept derived from that which distinguished the 'Industrial Revolution' in technology in recent European history, spoke of the 'Neolithic Revolution' and the 'Urban Revolution' as significant landmarks in this sequence.

Significant indeed these stages in social development certainly were, but an interesting state of affairs emerges when we compare the evidence derived from archaeology, and interpreted in terms of the technological-evolutionary and economic models of the past, with the evidence from the written record which exists for the later phases of the sequence. This was discussed by Henrs Frankfort in the instance of the two areas we have just mentioned, where archaeology and early history and literature combine to give a picture of the development of civilisation in two regions of the Near East. Archaeologically the two sequences seem to move along closely similar lines; we see a parallel development in technology from stone-using to metal-using societies, the increase in agricultural techniques which enabled the growth of larger static settlements, and the emergence of the town as a unit. But when we turn to consider the total body of evidence—archaeological and historical—which we have for the form, the character, the individual and unique quality of Mesopotamian civilisation by say 2000 B.C., and then compare this with what we similarly know of Egypt at the same time, we see not uniformity, but disparity. Each civilisation has achieved identity and individuality on a basis of common technology.

The evidence from written documents on social organisation, life, thought and belief, on all the aspects of the human past which are hardly if at all expressed in real archaeological evidence, enable us to apply a valuable corrective to the viewpoint which results from using only those models of the past applicable to such evidence. We can recognise in a civilisation, said Frankfort, 'a certain coherence among its various manifestations, a certain consistency in its orientation, a certain cultural "style" which shapes its political and its judicial institutions, its art as well as its literature, its religions as well as its morals'. But we can only recognise these qualities when our source-material includes the written record as well as that of material culture; it is possible for history, but not for prehistory.

The archaeologist working in historical fields has then the advantage over the prehistorian in that he can use all his resources of technique in the recovery and interpretation of material evidence, with the added possibility that, joined with the literary evidence, he can see the economic and technological aspects of what in prehistory would be no more than an abstract 'culture', in terms of a 'civilisation'. The archaeological models of the past tend to be concerned with, and to demonstrate, uniform processes common to large numbers of societies, but the possible (and indeed likely) diversity in what Frankfort called the 'form' of the societies can hardly be perceived by such means, and may in fact be obscured. It is when one has the knowledge of a society's 'form' derived from its written texts added to the archaeological evidence that one can perceive its individuality within an historical model of the past.

In the ancient Oriental civilisations we have been discussing, archaeological techniques have contributed practically all we know of the material achievements of the peoples concerned; their architecture and sculpture, the lay-out of town and temple, the crafts of the potter, the worker in bronze or precious metals and of the jeweller and seal-cutter. Refinements in techniques have given added knowledge of perishable substances, such as the solid-wheeled carts of Kish or Ur, where Sir Leonard Woolley similarly recovered the forms of the famous harps and other wooden objects, or the chariots of about 300 B.C. surviving as 'ghosts' in the soil in the Honan province in China. Indeed the similarly surviving traces of the Sutton Hoo boat of the seventh century A.D. in Suffolk, an instance of archaeological techniques operating in the field of early medieval history, could be quoted here as an example of the way in which the techniques of archaeological field-work may in any period or place illuminate the past by the recovery of unexpected objects or structures.

Although the co-operative approach of archaeologists and natural scientists has been employed with notable success in Western Asiatic prehistory, much more could be done in the historical field, here and in classical lands. On comparatively few oriental excavations up to the present has there been a treatment of the animal and plant remains from sites within the literate periods of antiquity on the comprehensive lines carried out for instance in the pioneer work half a century ago on the prehistoric site of Anau in Turkestan, or the full study of the animal remains from the Indus Valley city of Harappa. Here is a considerable field where ecological and environmental studies should be conducted as a necessary part of any excavation. In the Mediterranean the problems concerned with the changing environment brought about by human activity in ancient times, whereby lands originally forested have been denuded by man and goats to their present state, could with advantage be studied with a co-operative approach involving archaeologists, ancient historians, palaeobotanists and zoologists.

Classical archaeology, however, is still (as we have seen) suffering from having been established as a field of study at a time when it could only be conceived as art-history, so that works of art became an end in themselves. The dead weight of this tradition is still felt, and aspects of material culture other than works

I

of art or architecture remain Cinderella-studies to many scholars engaged on the study of the classical world. Much remains to be learnt, by archaeological means, of ancient technology and workshop processes, of the types of tools made and used, the agricultural systems employed, the exploitation of natural resources such as marble and other fine building-stones, as well as mining and metal-working techniques. Some work has of course been done—the marbles used in statuary and architecture have indeed received recent study involving their petrological determination and therefore their place of origin, on lines exactly analogous to those used on the similar problem of the sources of stones used for early second millennium axe-blades in the British Isles, as noticed in Chapter II. So too we shall see shortly that similar work has now been carried out in connection with English medieval buildings.

As the classical world constantly impinged on that of the non-literate barbarians around its edges, much of the archaeology of the Greek and Roman provinces becomes necessarily bound up with that of the 'prehistoric' peoples. The Greek colonies in the west, for instance, were after all not founded in uninhabited lands, nor did the Roman Empire incorporate the province of Britain as an island destitute of population. The student of classical archaeology in any area outside the metropolitan centres must be constantly involved in a consideration of the relations between the indigenous population and the bearers of Greek or Roman culture; relations which are to some extent reflected in literary sources but to a far greater degree can be perceived by archaeological evidence.

Roman Britain affords a good example of a field of classical archaeology which throughout its lifetime has been closely linked with the archaeology of the 'natives'—with what in terms of British prehistory would be the Iron Age cultures at the time of, and during, the Roman Occupation. Any consideration of the agricultural economy of Roman Britain must be based on an understanding of the archaeological evidence for the state of affairs in the centuries before the Conquest, and indeed the elucidation of the agrarian history of the centuries of Roman occupation has to use archaeological evidence throughout, with the scantiest gleanings from literary sources. So too the affairs of the military zone of the Province depend heavily on archaeological, rather than wholly literary, sources for their study, and our concept of Roman Britain would be an unrealistic one if we forgot that throughout the Occupation there were non-literate, 'prehistoric' peoples beyond the frontiers in Scotland and Ireland.

It is interesting to notice that in fact the development of archaeological techniques as applied to the classical world has been greater in the provinces than at the centre of the Empire. The very close dating of certain types of Roman pottery in the early centuries A.D. which enables us to use it almost like coinage, was worked out not in Italy (where much of it was in fact manufactured), but in the northern provinces, and now strata in an excavation in Rome itself may well find themselves dated by a pottery typology worked out from evidence in the Roman frontier-forts in Germany. The poor quality of Romano-British art is often deplored—'not merely the common vulgar ugliness of the Roman empire, but a blundering, stupid ugliness that cannot even rise to the level of that vulgarity', said Collingwood in a famous passage. But even if we feel like that about it, we may reflect that the lack of a high artistic achievement in the classical tradition within the British Province may have resulted in a compensatory broadening of the basis of our local version of classical archaeology, rather than a narrowing of its scope into a restricted field of art-history.

The transition from the application of archaeological techniques to the Roman world, into that of the sub-Roman and post-Roman phases, and so into the Middle Ages, is an obvious one. And in fact it is immediately apparent that when, with the collapse of classical civilisation in the West, the historical sources become less frequent and more unreliable, archaeological evidence will bulk large in the study of those disturbed centuries. This of course is the case. The Teutonic settlement of England from the middle fifth century A.D. onwards has a scanty enough historical documentation, and one full of ambiguities and difficulties: side by side with it we can place a mass of archaeological evidence, largely derived from the cemeteries of the invaders. Everyone acquainted with this field knows that the correlation between written history and archaeological evidence is of the greatest difficulty in certain instances, but nevertheless without the archaeology, the story of the coming of the Saxons and the subsequent settlement and consolidation would be a thin one indeed. In this field too we can make use of a discipline as yet hardly discussed in these pages, that of place-names.

The names of places, and more especially the names of natural features such as rivers, hills, promontories and estuaries, can have a long survival, and may embody elements of languages otherwise long extinct in the region. On the European continent and in the British Isles there survive names which not only go back to the time of the pre-Roman Celtic-speaking population, but in some instances may represent an even earlier stratum than that. The distribution of certain types of Celtic place-names has been used in conjunction with archaeology to demonstrate that one group must have been taken to Spain, for instance, by Celtic speakers fairly early in the first millennium B.C., and that others arrived at later dates in Britain. And in reconstructing the events of the Saxon invasion and settlement in England from the fifth century onwards, students of place-names work closely in collaboration with archaeologists and historians.

We have already seen that information on technological processes is by its very nature absent from early written records and similarly much of what went on under the wide heading of 'trade' did not become written until comparatively recent times, and often not then. The trade in Mediterranean wines with pre-Roman Britain is attested by the archaeological evidence of the amphorae, or jars in which it was shipped in bulk, the distribution of which show the main importers were the Belgic tribes of south-east England. In Roman times the trade of course increased and became general through the Province, but in the post-

Roman period archaeology shows the distinction between the beer-drinking Saxons in south-east England (with no evidence of imported amphorae), and the Celtic west, where the trade in Mediterranean and West French wines, at least for sacramental use and almost certainly for secular enjoyment as well, is evidenced again by amphorae of characteristic forms, and, with the slight documentary evidence for such trading activities, gives us the background of the medieval wine trade with Aquitaine.

Except for the relatively few surviving stone churches, our knowledge of building in Saxon England is almost wholly derived from archaeology. Particularly important have been the recent excavations which have revealed, by the application of the highest standard of techniques in the field, the plans and much of the constructional details of timber buildings of great size and magnificence of the sixth century A.D. and later, and at Yeavering in Northumberland have given us the complete lay-out of a royal palace-complex of quite remarkable interest: the palace of which Bede tells us, and where Paulinus baptised and preached to the Northumbrians for a month on end. Nor is it only in the Saxon period that archaeology is advancing our knowledge of timber buildings in the Middle Ages of England, however, for Hope-Taylor, who excavated Yeavering, was also able to demonstrate for the first time in this country the nature of timber tower and defences which crowned the castle-mounds or mottes of Norman England, by an excavation which satisfactorily enough demonstrated in archaeological terms what was partially known from the stylised representations of such timber castles in the Bayeux Tapestry. Archaeology has again advanced our knowledge of stone-built churches and castles of the earlier Middle Ages in Britain, by the same method of petrographic examination of the stones used as we have noted more than once before, and so shown what quarries were worked, and what was the geographical range of their output.

The study of the typology and distribution of pottery has long been one of the chief branches of archaeology, and this approach, extended into the Saxon and medieval fields, has again

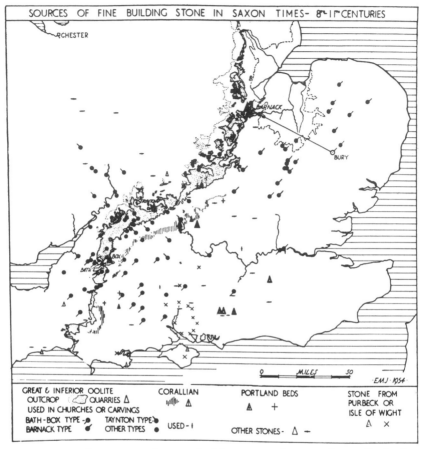

Fig. 12. The pattern of Saxon building materials in south-east England demonstrated by the same principles of petrographical examination as the prehistoric axe trade shown in Fig. 5.

enormously extended our knowledge of many aspects of trade, local manufactures, foreign contacts and internal communication-routes. In late Saxon times, for instance, we see pottery manufactured in the Cambridge-Bedford area being traded as far west as the Oxford region, and a whole range of foreign contacts with north France and the Rhineland, especially the latter region, demonstrated by imported wares in central and eastern England from Yorkshire to Hampshire; another ware of north German origin was popular in Cornwall, and its presence may well be connected with Viking trading activities. In the thirteenth century the distribution of fragments of fine painted wine-jugs manufactured in the region of Saintes in western France show, in their coastal distribution in Britain, from East Anglia and London, and round by the West Country to Wales and Galloway, the archaeological reflection of the wine trade once again, this time the trade with Gascony well attested in the documentary record.

It would be possible to give abundant additional examples of the application of archaeological techniques to historical cultures, both in the British Isles, here chosen as a convenient and illustrative area, and on the European continent and beyond. As I have tried to make it clear at many points in this book, archaeological techniques are capable of application to any field of history or prehistory, but only if the archaeologist works, not in isolation, but in the company of all those others, whose disciplines may lie in the sciences or the humanities, but who are concerned, in one way or another, with the study of the past of mankind.

CONCLUSIONS

AT the end of this brief survey of current practice and problems in archaeology, what sort of general conclusions can we put together? In the first place, I hope I have made it clear that our knowledge and perception of what constitutes the human past is dependent on various methods of approach, or techniques, all of which can be combined in the term 'history' in its wider sense. Of these means of approach to the past, archaeology is that which uses the unconscious evidence provided by the material remains surviving from antiquity, whether these are the products of communities with a written record, or without it. The discipline of archaeology has its own potentialities and its own limitations, its peculiar problems and its own rules of evidence and inference. Although closely allied to the discipline of the historian using documentary evidence, the nature of archaeological evidence dictates a distinctively different approach, especially when we are concerned with wholly or virtually non-literate peoples.

The view of the past which one can form is conditioned by the evidence from which this view is constructed, especially as meaningful arrangements of the phenomena observed can only be made within the framework of some sort of conceptual model which will permit of their interpretation. The models used when dealing with archaeological evidence have to be largely technological, evolutionary and economic, because it is these aspects of history which are reflected in the material culture which forms the archaeologist's subject-matter, and in the absence of historical documents archaeological evidence on its own will necessarily tend to produce a materialist view of the past, simply owing to the nature of the evidence available within this particular discipline. A recognition of the nature of the evidence in the archaeological approach to the past, as in all other approaches, is necessary because one can only frame questions to be investigated (and if possible answered), in terms of this evidence.

To obtain the basic data from which an archaeological view of the past can be constructed, an elaborate series of techniques have to be used, often involving a close co-operation with the disciplines of the pure and natural sciences, and, in historically documented contexts, with the humanistic disciplines as well. Archaeological techniques of recovery and interpretation are elaborate only because, once again, the nature of accidentally surviving evidence is such that its imperfections have to be countered where-ever possible, and its limited potentialities extended. This applies especially to the techniques of recovery and record, but after this has been achieved the subsequent interpretation and inference from the basic evidence has to follow rules applicable to this evidence.

All enquiries into the past are of their nature chronological—they involve the time dimension. Historical dates, obtained in the long run from documentary sources of some kind, are one kind of date, providing a more or less precise sequence in terms of solar years, or even in subdivisions of years. Archaeological dates may be relative—arrangements within a sequence which may at one or two points be tied to a 'true' date—or they may be absolute, and like the historical reckoning, expressed in terms of actual years. But owing to the fact that no written record extends back beyond about 3000 B.C., dates before that time must either be wholly inferential, or derived from natural time-scales operating independently of any human computations. Relative chronologies in archaeology can be worked out from archaeological evidence alone, but absolute chronologies can only be obtained either from a link-up with a historically documented sequence at long or close range, or determined by physical means such as that based on the radio-active breakdown of a carbon isotope. The latter method can be used throughout a very long span of human existence, continuing through the historical period, the former obviously only when contacts with written history in some form or other are possible.

For peoples who existed wholly before any written history or who constituted non-literate societies side by side with the ancient civilisations, archaeology alone can inform us of their very existence. Any knowledge we can have of the so-called pre-historic peoples is therefore that obtained from archaeological techniques, with all their limitations. But the term 'prehistoric' in current usage has an imprecise application, for there are whole series of gradations from absolute prehistory, before any written record existed anywhere, through varying degrees of proximity or relationship between non-literate and literate communities in the past. But essentially, for the non-literate communities archaeological evidence is all that is available, though it has to be used differently in accordance with the relationship which existed between the community under review and historical communities. Since in non-literate societies we have no knowledge of language or of nomenclature, we have to invent labels for the assemblages of material culture which we recognise as entities, and give an incon-sistent archaeological notation to the anonymous peoples we study.

The archaeological approach to the past is not however con-fined to non-literate societies. For people who possessed, in some form or other, an historical record, archaeological techniques can be used to illuminate aspects of life, such as technology, and subsistence-economics, which may be hardly, or not at all docu-mented in a strictly historical sense. The application of the archaeological techniques of typology and stylistic comparison to the field of works of art and architecture enables sequences and groupings to be established which may be called those of art-history, but which are arrived at by processes common to all study of material culture. Using a wider range of techniques than is possible within a single discipline, the co-operation of historians with the allied humanistic studies such as linguistics and archaeo-logy, as well as those of the natural sciences such as botany and zoology, can bring to bear on the study of the past of mankind a powerful team, representing more than one approach to the common problem, and envisaging it within the framework of more than one conceptual model. Within such a diversity, there is at least a possibility of a unity emerging.

SUGGESTIONS FOR FURTHER READING

FOR those who may wish to follow up some of the main points made in this book, and to pursue certain matters further, some of the more important books (and occasional papers in technical journals) are listed here. For Chapter I, general discussions of the nature of archaeology and its place in the wider study of the past of mankind have been made in such books as O. G. S. Crawford, *Man and His Past* (1921), V. G. Childe, *Piecing together the Past* (1956), R. G. Collingwood, *An Autobiography* (1939), and *The Idea of History* (1946). S. J. de Laet, *Archaeology and Its Problems* (1957), covers much of the ground I have also traversed in this book, at greater length and from the viewpoint of a Continental archaeologist. The story of the invention and earlier application of the technological model of the Stone, Bronze and Iron Ages has been given, with critical comment, by G. E. Daniel, *The Three Ages* (1943), and the nature and limitations of archaeological evidence has been discussed by C. F. C. Hawkes in a paper on 'Archaeological Theory and Method: Some suggestions from the Old World', published in *The American Anthropologist*, Vol. 56 (1954). Further comments on this aspect are contained in M. A. Smith's paper, 'The Limitations of Inference in Archaeology', published in *The Archaeological News Letter*, Vol. 6 (1955). The technical results of the Wessex Bronze Age investigation described on pp. 17-21 was published as 'The Early Bronze Age in Wessex', in *Proceedings of the Prehistoric Society*, Vol. 4, (1938); Wheeler's Wessex and North French campaigns are published in *Maiden Castle Dorset* (1943) and *Hill-Forts of Northern France* (1957), and the Indian research in a series of papers published in *Ancient India*, Nos. 2 (1946), 4 (1947-8) and 5 (1949).

There are many books dealing with archaeological techniques, and we may begin with R. J. C. Atkinson, *Field Archaeology* (1953), Wheeler's *Archaeology from the Earth* (1954), and J. G. D. Clark, *Archaeology and Society* (1957). Field-work, with particular application to southern England, is the subject-matter of O. G. S. Crawford, *Archaeology in the Field* (1953): there is much about air-photography in this book, and its wider application is demonstrated by J. S. P. Bradford, *Ancient Landscapes* (1957). Techniques other than those of excavation and field-work are discussed in Childe's *Piecing together the Past*, already referred to. The co-operation with the natural scientists forms the subject-matter of many technical reports, but the results are best seen on a wide front in J. G. D. Clark's *Prehistoric Europe: The Economic Basis* (1952), while the methods of pollen-analysis are demonstrated for the British Isles in H. Godwin, *History of the British Flora* (1956). The Star Carr site is published in J. G. D. Clark's monograph, *Star Carr* (1954), and he summarised the earlier work on the North German sites in a paper in *Antiquity*, Vol. 12 (1938). The development of excavation and interpretative techniques, including those of Montelius, are described by G. Bibby, in *The Testimony of the Spade* (1957). An excellent summary of recent work in this country is contained in *Recent Archaeological Excavations in Britain*, edited by R. L. S. Bruce-Mitford (1956).

The questions of constructing time-scales, especially those involving the natural sciences, are fully dealt with by F. Zeuner, in his *Dating the Past* (1958), by Childe in *Piecing together the Past* and by Bibby in *The Testimony of the Spade*. Godwin's *History of the British Flora* gives a summary of the pollen-zones and their dating so far as the British Isles are concerned. Claude Schaeffer put forward his theory of earthquake correlations in his *Stratigraphie comparée et Chrononologie de l'Asie Occidentale* (1948), and attempted to correlate the Enkomi flooding with Northern Europe in *Enkomi-Alasia I* (1952).

Books describing the use of archaeology in the investigation of prehistoric societies are of course innumerable: Clark's *Prehistoric Europe: the Economic Basis* shows what can be achieved for that region by archaeological means. He defined the concept of 'primary prehistory' in his inaugural lecture, *The Study of Prehistory* (1954), and the relationship between archaeology and the disciplines of the natural sciences on the one hand, and the humanities on the other, was discussed at length by C. F. C. Hawkes in his address, 'Archaeology as Science: Purposes and Pitfalls', published in *The Advancement of Science*, No. 54 (1957). Childe made his classic definition of an archaeological culture, and discussed its implications, in *The Danube in Prehistory* (1929). The problems in grouping cultural units in Neolithic Britain are set out in my *Neolithic Cultures of the British Isles* (1954), and some of the aspects of the problems connected with chambered tombs also discussed by me in a paper, 'Architecture and Ritual in Megalithic Monuments', published in the *Journal of the Royal Institute of British Architects*, 3rd Series, No. 63 (1956).

For a study of a people involving an inter-disciplinary approach from the standpoints of archaeology, history and linguistics, T. G. E. Powell's *The Celts* (1958) shows admirably how such a task has to be undertaken. The questions of conditional literacy were recently brought up in connection with the Linear B script by S. Dow, 'Minoan Writing', in the *American Journal of Archaeology*, Vol. 58 (1954), and by K. H. Jackson in the instance of the Celtic and Latin languages in this country in his *Language and History in Early Britain* (1953), from which quotation is made. The principles governing the stratification of *tells* and similar sites are fully presented by Wheeler, *Archaeology from the Earth*, and the contrasting schemes obtained by using a technological as well as an historical model for the same region come out in two books on Anatolia—S. Lloyd, *Early Anatolia* (1956) and O. R. Gurney, *The Hittites* (1952). The archaeological and linguistic problems of the Indo-European languages are set out in H. Hencken, *Indo-European Languages and Archaeology* (1955) and in a paper by R. A. Crossland, 'Indo-European Origins: the Linguistic Evidence', in *Past and Present*, No. 12 (1957). The divergent characters of the Mesopotamian and Egyptian civilisations are demonstrated by H. Frankfort in *The Birth of Civilisation in the Near East* (1951); the quotation on Romano-British art by

R. G. Collingwood is from his *Roman Britain and the English Settlements* (with J. N. L. Myres) (1936). B. Hope-Taylor's Yeavering excavations are not yet published, but the timber structures on the motte are described in *Recent Archaeological Excavations in Britain*, Chapter 10. In the same volume the distribution of some types of Saxon pottery are discussed by R. L. S. Bruce-Mitford in Chapter 8; others by C. A. R. Radford and G. C. Dunning in *Dark-Age Britain* (1956).

INDEX

Catalog

If you are interested in a list of fine Paperback
books, covering a wide range of subjects
and interests, send your name and address,
requesting your free catalog, to:

McGraw-Hill Paperbacks
330 West 42nd Street
New York, New York 10036